SUPER ACCELERATED LIVING

SUPER ACCELERATED LIVING

How to Manifest an Epic Life

BENTINHO MASSARO

Janet Marchant, *Editor*

SUPER ACCELERATED LIVING

Published by
Trinfinity Publishing
Boulder, Colorado

For information address: Trinfinity Corp., Post Office
Box 12, Boulder, CO 80306

Trinfinity Corp.: http://trinfinity.us
Trinfinity Academy: http://trinfinityacademy.com

ISBN 978-0-692-80530-5

Everything depends on how much you care about your existence. If you care about being alive, if you're excited about the potential that this life offers you, then you'll start to ask the right questions and stumble upon teachings like these. If you care about your life, if you care about not going through your life un-consciously any longer, if you care about what's possible for your short time here on Earth, you will take huge leaps in your expansion simply reading through these pages. If you want what truly matters and you're done with lesser goals, this book is for you. There is no time to waste. Be open-minded and activate your endless potential. Set your spiritual—and material—path ablaze with the fire of *Super Accelerated Living*.

- Bentinho Massaro

Contents

Introduction

In the first weeks of 2015, a watershed year for the expansion of his teachings, Bentinho Massaro gave a series of breakthrough meetings on personal empowerment and manifestation. "If you follow these guidelines *to the T*," he said, "your life gets crazy."

The meetings were remarkable, intensely charged, challenging, and even lovingly aggressive at times, all focused on explaining how manifestation works—*and that it actually does work.*

Recently, he decided to combine three of these meetings into a book, saying it would **make for a very powerful manual for living an epic life.**

His goal is to help people effectively use their innate power and the Law of Attraction to radically upgrade their lives. He sees this upgrade happening on both the individual and global scale, and maintains the vision of transforming humanity to an enlightened civilization within our lifetime. All individuals who raise their personal frequency, he explains, will substantially contribute to this process, even if invisible or unknown to themselves.

Bentinho Massaro is the leading synthesizer of Law of Attraction teachings from many sources both current and historical, and he is unique in combining empowerment techniques with enlightenment teachings—to create a balanced, loving, and conscious human experience. His online platform, Trinfinity Academy, provides courses on both Self-Realization (enlightenment) and Self-Actualization (empowerment) as these two lines of development enhance and catalyze one another.

Therefore, this book is not simply a bag of tricks for manifesting a Maserati or a mansion (although it teaches you how to do that, too). It guides readers to access their true creative powers through expanding their Presence and Awareness as well as their capacity for love, appreciation, gratitude, and service. The methods and practices presented here are designed to be received *experientially*, not just by the intellect.

- Janet Marchant, Ed.

Part I:

Become a Manifestation Powerhouse

"Are you ready for the most powerful shift in attitude and attention in your life? Are you ready for the turning point? Are you ready to leave behind the thought that you are the receiver of reality and realize fully that you are a God —the creator of reality? If not, don't watch tonight's meeting for it will most likely only confuse you."

- Bentinho Massaro

In this meeting, Bentinho shares one of his most powerful techniques for tapping into our unlimited, *innate* power to create our own reality. Not for the faint of heart, these tools are for willing and ready, conscious creators only.

He emphasizes the essential point that if we wish to overcome a lifetime of unconscious, undirected manifesting, we need to become highly deliberate— almost forceful—in the sheer power of our Presence— to attain a "super-high, finely tuned Presence and intentional state of Love-Light."

He explains why it is crucial to avoid focusing on results, but to remain unflinching in the face of whatever appears. "Not once do you flinch," he says.

"Internally, subjectively, your state of being is 100% your chosen preference all of the time. As soon as you start choosing only your preferred experience, your reality will have to reflect that."

* * * * *

This meeting was streamed live on January 5, 2015 in Boulder, Colorado.

*　*　*　*　*

A few disclaimers

This topic is a bit radical so I will offer a couple of disclaimers.

First of all, this may or may not immediately hit home for you; it may not immediately become experiential. When it does become experiential, *it will shift your sense of identity 180 degrees*! It will shift your sense of who you are, where you come from, and what you can do. It is powerful stuff.

The second disclaimer for this topic is that it assumes you are already at a certain level of, shall we say, purity—purity of mind, a certain centeredness. It assumes you have already explored the tricks your mind plays on you and are aware of how it acts up. It assumes that you have worked on this and have transformed and transcended many of your mind-based misconceptions. So, my sharing of this material at this time assumes that you've done this work to the extent that your intention is by now very aligned— very highly aligned to Spirit, to Abundance, to Love, to being an unconditional vessel of the Creator.

It assumes you are aware of yourself beyond the "personal bubble," beyond the bubble of "I am this body, I am this mind, this is what I need to get...and everyone else can suck on it." It assumes that those games of comparison and insecurity have, to a great extent, been seen through (though not necessarily completely eradicated), and that you are already a rather balanced, finely-tuned vehicle of the Infinite. (If that is not the case, that's absolutely fine, too—just see what hits home for you, and see what does not.)

A third potential disclaimer is that some of this material, to an unprepared audience, may seem "egotistical." It may sound arrogant; it may sound like it is driven by the personal self. That's why I said it assumes you've seen through some of these personal bubbles. And, further, that you've seen through some of the *spiritual* bubbles, meaning the ideas of what the "ego" is and that you must hammer the ego down, and all of that stuff.

For people without such a background, this topic may seem like it's coming from a place of manipulation or domination or overpowering things with your personal will. But this is not where it's coming from. This is not what it's telling you to do.

To help avoid such misunderstandings, I'll be reminding you from time to time about how to maintain integrity while applying these ideas to your life.

Are you the receiver or the creator of 'reality'?

I want you now to imagine what it would be like to never, ever *receive* anything again. What would it be like to not have the feeling, or the sense, that you are at the receiving end of Creation? Yes, you are *perceiving* Creation, but are you really *receiving* Creation?

What if you are *not* receiving Creation, and what if that was never the case? What if 100% of the time, every nanosecond, the billions of molecules that make up the universe were placed there by you? What if you are the *conceiver* and the *giver* of experiences...that it's *you* who gives Creation its form? What if you're not a mind-body walking around in a predetermined physical, external reality, but rather that all of this is your own manifestation?

Now, this may not be a completely new concept to you—the idea that we create our reality—but what might be slightly new to you is the more radical approach of recognizing that you have never, *ever* received anything. You have always created this moment; you have always decided how this moment is going to appear. And, *you can become conscious of this once again!*

Instead of being an *unconscious* creator, believing you are the receiver of your own creations, you can step back fully into the Creator seat—by becoming more conscious as well as more deliberate. You can take back the reins. This is not about control—at least not in the way we have turned control into a negative concept. It is about control in terms of *conscious creation*. You take control of *yourself*. You become more deliberate in your manifestations.

Feel into the fact that you have never received Creation—*ever*. Really feel into it, because there is an endless depth to feeling into this. It is not like, "Oh yeah... I get the idea. That's a fun idea." No. If you feel into it, it starts to become real and it shifts your paradigm. So again, for a moment, feel into the fact that you have never ever received Creation, that you have always created every single detail of what you perceive. *There is no giver of experiences other than you.* No-one and nothing has ever given you an experience; you have never been on the receiving end of Creation.

What if that were true? What if this dream reality has always already been 100% your manifestation—every single detail of it? Not just how you respond to things, but the things themselves; this very chair that I'm sitting on is *you* placing it under my butt. All the time, billions of times per second, you are placing the chair underneath me. What if it was *you doing* that? What if you were not receiving that? What if this was not external to you—what if there is *no external reality whatsoever*?

Step one – Try it out! Play with the idea of no external reality

Here's where it gets interesting. The shift becomes practicable and experiential when you start to play with this concept, when you *try it out*.

Start experimenting with ignoring the sense that there is a reality outside of yourself—which has become a sense perception through automatic conditioning. But just ignore that sense; practice ignoring everything, ignoring everyone. And imagine the absence of the feeling that you are walking around in an actual physical world. Eliminate that for a moment; press the eject button—gone!

For just a moment...sense that there is no external reality. There has never been a reality "out there." There has never been another person you have interacted with. There has never been an actual physical world that you have been a part of. You are not a *part* of anything. You are the Creator of the *entirety* of the Universe, of All-That-Is.

What if everything is completely, 100% subjective?

Feel into the sense, that you can create right now, of me being "over here," external to you. Just look at me and feel into that sense—which is very automatic and is normally naturally there. This is how we tend to perceive our surroundings; this is the vibration from which we tend to perceive reality. The underlying assumption is that there is a reality over there, and I'm over here.

Even the idea, "I create my reality," is still dominated by the sense and the underlying assumption that you are walking around in a sandbox that exists independent of your consciousness, independent of you, independent of your creation. You still think, "Okay, within this *actual* sandbox, I can start attracting everything I desire. I can start creating things that are beautiful and filled with love and light."

But even this is a flawed concept. The sandbox within which you seem to be playing is already *placed there by you* in this very second; it is not *actually* there. You are not walking around in something that already exists. The entirety of the Universe is walking around *in you*. But only because you choose for that to be the case. Why? Because you are a god—literally.

Again, feel into that automatic sense of that person is over there. Notice the feeling of distance and the feeling of difference; notice the feeling of me being external to you and of you having an internal world inside of your bubble. Notice the feeling of me being outside of your bubble. Feel how you are navigating your bubble through this world with other beings and objects and realities and stars. Just feel that for a moment and notice how you can actually feel the sense perception within your own consciousness of there being an external reality. Can you feel that? The more clearly you can identify, or pinpoint, in your consciousness the sense that there is an external reality, the more easily you can then ignore it or block it out.

Now, shift to completely ignoring the sense of an external reality, if you can. When you block external reality out, what you're doing is no longer creating an illusion; it's not that you are blocking out something that actually exists. The sense that there is an external reality is an illusion to begin with, so you can safely ignore it. You can safely block it out because it's not real. *All you're doing is ceasing to generate the illusory sense that there is a world outside of yourself.*

What are you left with when you ignore or disregard external reality? How does your sense perception change? How does your state of consciousness shift its sense of identity? When you stop referencing an outside world, when you stop feeling like there is anything but your presence—anything but your preference, anything but your state of being, anything but that which *you* see—how does that shift things?

You can practice going back and forth if you want. You can notice, "Oh, that person is outside of me." And then go back to the viewpoint of dismissing that perception and notice the feeling of non-physicality that you're left with—the spaciousness, the state of being of the Creator seat. This is your Creator Space; it's your Holodeck, your Creation Station. What if you could be in this state, practically speaking, all the time, or at least most of the time? What if you stopped referencing anything beyond *your* vision, beyond *your* creation, beyond *your* consciousness?

What if you simply stopped referencing all of that and changed your relationship to the things you see and to the people you meet? Instead of saying, "Oh, these are external creatures," start saying, "These are my manifestations—manifestations of my own essence, of my own being. They are being placed here by me. They are puppets. They are creations. They are amazing creations of the One that I am!"

Step two – *Insist* on seeing only your preferred reality

Since all there is is you, you can start to shape your reality. You can paint it. You can overpower it, overwhelm it with your chosen preference, until all you see—regardless of what you're looking at—is what you prefer. Until all you see is who you choose to be in that moment. Until all you see is the frequency you choose to overwhelm your creation with. Feel into that for a moment. What if all you experience in this moment is the frequency, or the preference, you choose to experience?

You can practice this with anyone. You can look at someone speaking, and instead of seeing him speak, you completely ignore that and see only what you prefer to see. Try it out. You can do this with anything.

As you practice in this way, your experience becomes more and more a non-physical, instantaneous presence that you experience, that is then *colored by you*. It's not just the generic "Presence" that everyone speaks about like, "Oh yeah, let's all be present." Of course it *is* that, because that's what everything is. But in this case it's infused or colored by you, consciously and specifically. It is infused with the Creator that you are. It's not just a receptive state of being; it's a *manifesting state of being*. It is an actionable state of being, a constant Presence-Creatorship state of being.

You look at someone and you overpower them with what you prefer to see. You ignore them completely for a moment. *This is where it becomes a little radical*, because it conflicts with some of our ideas of what it's like to be social, what it's like to be respectful and to honor the other person. But for the purpose of practice, completely overpower the person, completely ignore who they are, who you think they are, and what they might be saying. Paste onto that person your preferred state so that all you see is your preference—whatever that is, whatever you want that person to be, whatever you want to experience yourself as. Maintain that presence as you look at the person and create—or generate—an energy there. Generate a presence that is of your preference.

So you're not receiving. You're not waiting. You're not judging the scenario. You're not anticipating what's occurring. You are actually *generating* what that scenario is going to be like. You're not in the state of, "Oh, there's an actual scenario out there that I need to somehow listen to or adjust myself to."

This does not mean there's no respect or integrity. As I said in the disclaimers, assuming that you have reached a certain level of purity and integrity, you already know what it's like to be compassionate and loving. So given the fact that you have mastered that to some extent, you can now practice these techniques and notice that you can actually paste onto someone whatever you want, and that person will *turn into that*. Why? Because that person is not here!

It's not that the person changes. It's not that you manipulate who that person is, or that you don't listen to who that person is. What actually happens is that **you become conscious for the first time of what you have already been unconsciously doing anyway.**

When you were thinking you were respecting the other person by being in a receptive state of, "Oh, there's an actual person over there," *you were already generating that person.* But because of your doubts and your hesitancies, you were generating them in confused ways. You were generating that relationship in ways that were not of your preference—but it was *you* doing that. You were *already* placing them there.

Now, as you start practicing this, it might feel radical, outside-of-the-box, and even unsocial to an extent. For a period of time, it may feel strange to your mind's belief system. *But what you're actually doing, mechanically or energetically speaking, is becoming conscious of what you are already doing anyway.*

As you start practicing *consciously*, and then actually generating things that pop up in your reality, at first it may feel like, "It's me overpowering my reality, it's me dominating my reality, it's me spilling over and bombarding my experience with the frequency of my choice." But that is only the initial sense. At some point, you realize that *that's how Creation works.* The sense of, "I am over here overpowering this," starts to dissolve, and it all becomes an inseparable, singular creation. You realize every moment that this is what you are now painting in the picture. If you have ever had a lucid dream, it's no different than this.

Step Three – Amp up to super-high presence, to Your God Frequency

Practice this right now with me. Paste onto me whatever you want me to be. What would you prefer that I be? What would the relationship between you and me ideally be like? *Force* that upon me. I need to use forceful words because we have assumed that we are victims for so long. Since you are stuck in a state that's not real, stuck in the sense that you are separate from your reality, I need to counter that with a word like "force."

So, energetically, *force* upon me what you desire me to be; leave me no choice to be any other way. Be very sincere in this practice and aware of your integrity. And be in your Presence. This is not just a thought, it is *Presence!* You have to overpower what is appearing with Presence; you have to manifest and generate the experience you want *consciously.* Because that's where we generate reality from—from a state of super-high, fine-tuned Presence, from a high-frequency state. So, you need to match that frequency in order to get results and in order to become more conscious of the fact that this is what you are doing all the time.

You are God. *You are God!* You are nothing else but God. So, look at me—or anything that appears to you—and overwhelm me with *you*. What would you prefer me to be? (I start undressing, I start dancing... haha.) But you see, even if I *don't* do the thing you're demanding me to do or become, that doesn't change a single thing for you! All you keep seeing is your preference. All you keep feeling is your preference. In your mind, in your consciousness, I am still what you desire me to be—no matter how I act, no matter what I say, no matter how doubtful it may seem, no matter how unsuccessful your generation may seem. *That does not matter to you!* You still see and perceive your preference; you still dominate your reality with your preference. All you see is your preference.

This is actually one of the most powerful keys to becoming conscious again of the fact that you are a god, that you are a creator: it's to actually *practice* overpowering and overwhelming your reality with your chosen presence, your chosen frequency. Then you will really fall in love with your reality, with your creation. You will start to become one with it, rather than *thinking* there is unity, but still *feeling* like you're a victim of an external reality.

And remember...when you practice forcing your preference upon your reality, it doesn't mean you lose your integrity and do whatever the fuck you want to people; that's not what I'm saying. What I'm saying is that you overpower your experience of what-is with only your preference, while maintaining *complete respect* for the seeming existence of other people's free will. At the same time, all you see and experience is your preference, regardless of how people respond, regardless of what they say. This not only works for relationships, it works for anything—for your career, for any project or event you want to generate, for your everyday experiences, for your body, for the way you want to feel, and so on.

Regardless of what appears, you can choose to see and manifest and generate *only* your preferred state. Now, initially, it may feel like you are overpowering your "reality." That's okay. Just practice and get the hang of it. Instead of asking, "What is this reality all about?" you *decide* what it's all about! Then...*that's what it is all about!* So, there's your answer: you are here to be a creator, not a victim. We are all lost sheep. We have forgotten the fact that we are gods and goddesses.

We are not here to find things out, not really. Yes, this existence is about learning, but we're not really here to discover things, as such. We are here to *create* things that have never been created before. We are here to generate. How do we generate? We generate according to our true desires, according to our true inspiration. Not just, "I want a lot of money so I won't have debt." Not those types of preferences; they are irrelevant. (Although, you can practice with those, as well—that's fine.)

But what I'm talking about is a really high, <u>finely-tuned intentional state of Love-Light</u> that can have any shape. The diamond of Love-Light has many facets. It can be bliss. It can be excitement. It can be inspiration, or love, or compassion, or integrity. It can be sincerity or joy—whatever is your highest excitement! Choose one of the facets of that high vibrational Love-Light of the One Infinite Creator, tap into it, and dominate your reality with it.

Don't care what anyone else thinks. Don't care what they say or how they act. Again, this doesn't mean that you're not present to other beings: it simply means that all you focus on and generate is the mind state and energy state of your preference. And it doesn't mean that others have to act in certain ways. But you will see that when you start exuding your preference—and when it's really in alignment with your Higher Self and their Higher Selves—that they *do* start responding to your energy. Not because you told them to, not because you dominated them—but because you *generated the frequency* that took you into the parallel reality where the highest option, in the best interest of "both of you" is now becoming manifest.

How it works – How you create your world from your own energy

How did you manifest that parallel reality? You did it *by being all-in,* by not doubting your power. It worked because you didn't hesitate, you didn't doubt or fall back into the role of seeker, questioning your power. You didn't accept the idea of an already-existent universe from which you have to take your cues. There *is* no universe that already exists that you have to take your cues from. That universe, my friends, does not exist. It has never, ever existed. It has been made up. By whom? By you.

You have created the illusion of an external reality that you feel you have to listen to. Within this illusion, you generated a focal point of a body-mind. And then you generated the thought that the focal point of the body-mind is somehow *not* the focal point of the environment, or of everything else. Thus you created the illusion of separation.

You generated lots of ideas about this separation. You thought, "If I want to be compassionate or honorable, I need to regard the reality outside of myself as the end-all and be-all. I have to listen to what mummy and daddy said. I have to pay attention to what happens to me from the outside world. If I don't, I'm being arrogant, I'm being egotistical." In actuality, *you* generate the effects from the inside out. *You* generate the other person. *You* generate the focal point of the body-mind with its sense of separation. There has never been that world that you feel is external to you, and never anything outside that you need to listen to. That is just a thought.

This is your *Creation*; it is not your "Reception." You are never receiving anything *ever*; you are only ever *giving* life to Creation. You are only ever using the unconditional love field that is the One Infinite Creator's desire to know itself, to express itself. This expression generated *you*—an autonomous I-AM that can then generate its own reality, and does so. But then, as a human being, you forget that you're doing this all the time. And so you generate yourself into a very isolated corner of "I am this versus that," forgetting that everything you can ever see is generated out of your own energy only.

You can never experience anyone else's energy, not truly. Yes, communication between worlds can happen and does happen all the time. We do co-create in that sense. However, your experience of co-creation with others is generated out of *your* energy solely, because you can't experience anything else. It is a mechanical impossibility to experience someone else's energy. It's always your version. It's your reflection of that communication, and it happens on a completely different level that I can't even begin to describe here.

True connection between spirits, between souls, between consciousnesses or I-AMs, is not what we think it is. It's not when I'm touching your body. It's not about when I'm feeling your heart open and my heart open and we have a beautiful connection. That is a physical reflection, or even a non-physical reflection, of the true connection *that is already beyond space-time.* Everything is generated within that inseparability of all souls that is really the One Soul interacting with itself, forgetting that it is one soul interacting with itself!

So, again, when you practice these methods, and you choose what you desire to become in this moment, do not focus on the results. Regardless of how things appear, regardless of how it reflects you, *do not flinch.* You do not flinch. Not once do you flinch. You can still communicate with others, but internally, subjectively, your state of being is 100% your chosen preference all of the time.

Take it beyond knowledge – Make it *experiential*

With some practice, you will remember that this is what you have always already been doing, and you'll start forgetting that there is such a thing as an external world. You become naturally, energetically, vibrationally one with the Universe. Rather than "seeking for spirituality" and understanding it from a very simple "Presence" point of view, you start to actually, vibrationally understand and know that *there is nothing but you.*

You want the experiential side of this, not just the knowledge of it. You want to *become* it. If you want to become it...then you need to become it! How do you become it? By doing what is *counter-intuitive.* You force yourself upon your Creation, because that's what you always already do, but you have forgotten that you do it. In order to taste that again consciously, you tap into your inspiration, you tap into a high vibrational Love-Light state and you paste it onto everything you see, disregarding everything you saw before.

This means that the things you perceive, like walking down Pearl Street in Boulder, are never going to be the same again. Because you're not going to look at

Pearl Street, you're not going to be the victim of Pearl Street, you're not going to be the *receiver* of Pearl Street. You're going to be *the creator* of Pearl Street. Pearl Street will look however you want it to look, and feel however you want it to feel. Pearl Street will respond to you in whatever way you desire your creation—and Pearl Street *is* your creation—to respond to you.

As I said, this may sound a little radical, and in a sense it is. And again, if you are not sure what to do, go for integrity. But you will find that true integrity does not conflict with generating the reality of your preference. If you ever have doubt, and you feel like you're about to do something crazy that might be against your integrity, take a deep breath, relax, and perhaps let go of the need to execute that desire. Don't suppress it, but simply take a break. Take a relaxing breath and tune into integrity first. And then let that guide you.

However, at a certain point you become naturally attuned, because you are increasing your frequency so that you *actually see more as Higher Self sees*, as Higher Consciousness sees. You interact and experience more as Higher Self does; you see much more of reality that is happening around you that most people are completely oblivious to. With all of that information at your disposal, you will know what integrity is. From that space, you will see that it's not conflicting to generate your reality, because that's what you are doing always, already anyway. And there is great love. Don't worry!

For those to whom this feels too radical, be assured that it's not a selfish state. Ultimately, it's not a selfish state because, honestly, it's the most *selfless* state. You become of service because you no longer feel separate. You become the Whole. You become *all* of your creation, not just your focal point inside of your creation. Your well-being is no longer limited to the focal point of your body-mind. Your well-being becomes whatever is entering your reality, whatever is generated inside of your reality. You care about the well-being of all of Creation. For me, this means that the well-being of all of you is actually my well-being. It's not just "my" well-being that is my well-being!

But you can't really know what that's like, you can't really know how to respond or interact from that space, you can't really recognize that integrity, *until you start actually experiencing it*. And you can only experience what it's like when you expand beyond your bubble, beyond your biases, beyond your preferences (the lower preferences, the idea of needs), and you remember your *true* preference.

Your true preference may be varied; it may be any form of the Love-Light expression that is the Infinite's most immediate expression of itself. We can translate this to be excitement, inspiration, passion, creativity, joy, co-creation, love, wisdom. Just take your version—whatever feels the most exciting and alive to you—and make that all you see, regardless of what's actually happening.

So, can you start practicing seeing only your own preference? The key to practicing this effectively is to start sensing a clear distinction between the two modes of being that you have access to (that we practiced together earlier). One mode is being a victim of a creation "out there." The other is realizing, experientially, that there *is* no creation out there. So you can say, "This is my creation; this is what I generated into being. I can feel my preference, and I can exude or extend that onto the rest of myself— which is my creation, my vision, my dream world, right here."

Practice alternating these modes. Shift back into the first, habitual mode: "Oh, but what about this circumstance, what about that?" You feel smaller and smaller. You feel more and more isolated, more and more separate. Then shift into your preferred creation mode: you feel expansive, nowhere and everywhere at the same time. You feel like you are energy. You feel like you are Consciousness.

So, start practicing this—referring only to your own preference. Disregard everything else. Ignore all other stimuli and all other impulses. Ignore all your habitual responses and thoughts, all of your unconscious habits. *Because the belief in an external reality is no more than a habit!* So create new habits: take your version of reality—whatever feels the most exciting, the most alive to you—and make that *all* that you see, regardless of what's actually happening.

It may seem counter-intuitive, but when you seriously take on the mode of overwhelming your creation with whatever you desire it to become— choosing your preferred frequency of being, pasting it onto your creation, and becoming oblivious to anything else—then things will be *revealed to you in your own direct experience.* And this is what you need. This is what you desire. Otherwise, it's just another concept and you will use it in erroneous ways.

(Again, this assumes that a high level of integrity and awareness is already present. Then the shift is not so radical because you know you can never, ever do anything that is truly out of alignment or integrity. You can't—you are too good; you are too balanced already. You know too much. You know that this is all your Self so you won't use it in selfish, erroneous ways.)

See as Higher Self sees

So, start practicing this—overwhelming your creation with your preferred frequency. Practice is necessary because you have practiced the opposite for so long! You need to counter what you've been doing for decades, which is: "I'm over here... you're over there." This is why you need to *overwhelm* your creation with your frequency so you can start to create more deliberately.

Initially it feels like, "Oh, wait a second, I am seeping out from my bubble into what's over there!" But when your frequency starts *blending more with life itself* (life outside your bubble) you start feeling, "I was never separate to begin with."

At this point, whatever frequency you cultivate will immediately seem to be part of the environment. Self and circumstances will be felt as non-separate, so that when overwhelming your environment it will feel more like you're changing *yourself* rather than trying to influence something outside yourself. Your chosen preference will appear more instantaneously, and you'll start seeing Creation as a non-physical field of energy.

This is your palette and your canvas; you can use it to create whatever you desire. Overwhelm yourself with this state until you *become* your environment, until you *become* your creation. In a dream it's easier to see this, especially if you are having a lucid dream or something close to it. You realize, "Wait—this is a dream!" It becomes easier to see that not only are you the body inside of the dream, you are actually *the whole dream.* Have you ever experienced that in a dream? You *are* the environment. You *are* the clouds you are flying towards. You're not just the body that is flying through the clouds—you are *actually* the clouds. You *are* the sun in the distance, all of these things. In the same way, you overpower your relationships—and by "relationships" I mean your relationship to the world, to things, to people, to money, to your dreams, to everything.

As soon as you start choosing only your preferred experience, your reality will *have to* reflect that, so you will feel more and more inseparable from your environment. It has to be this way *because your frequency goes so high that you start to see as Higher Self sees,* and Higher Self sees very naturally that all is its own Creation.

So you can stop thinking, "Oh, someone once said I'm All-That-Is. Well, that's a nice thought." If you think this way, you'll never "be all-in." But If you take this practice *all the way* vibrationally, if you really apply it, it can be an inspirational quality that becomes your preferred state of being. All you see is your preference. What is your preference? To know that you are All-That-Is. That's one example. You see, your preference doesn't have to be, "I want a lot of money so I can do everything I want." It can be simply be, "I-AM who I-AM, already. I-AM who I want to be already. I only see results. I only see success. I only see my preference. *Only!*"

Don't flinch. Don't doubt. As soon as you doubt...boom! That's the return of, "I am over here, you are over there." But if that happens, that's great, too, because you feel the contrast. "Oh, shit. I collapsed back into victimization." And the contrast to that is, "Oh my God—I feel so infinitely powerful!" It can be scary at first. It can be so scary that it collapses you back into feeling separate. And that's natural—don't judge yourself when that happens. This practice might sound a little intense, but that's only to counter what you have already been doing for so long.

And wherever you are with these practices is totally fine with me. I really have no preference for you because I see my own preference already, regardless of how you act, regardless of what you realize.

But from your viewpoint, it may be of compelling importance to learn how to dominate your reality because it is, in fact, *your* reality. You may feel drawn to make your personal commitment to "be all-in." The more you practice, the more effortless, natural, relaxed, and in integrity it becomes. You become more balanced. It doesn't become this idea of, "Oh, I can do whatever I want!" No, it's a really balanced Love-Light state; it's a pure high-frequency, balanced, Higher-Self-way of seeing life. And yes, it is infinitely powerful!

Going forward in your new life – Some final advice

Don't expect yourself to immediately succeed 100% with this practice, because it's not possible. Well, everything is possible, haha, but that's not going to happen. For me, this way of being continues to become more real every day. It becomes more applicable every day. It becomes more real for me every day.

There is no end to this journey. At some point, you will be every single molecule you create, but that's simply not relevant yet, because what's relevant is to have a *human* experience. If you were at that level, you would not be physical. You would be in a completely different form, beyond your comprehension, exploring what it would be like to actually become All-That-Is. But for us, it's relevant to explore this journey on the human scale, on this dimensional plane.

So, don't expect 100% success with this. But do expect yourself to become more aware of the *difference* between the victim state of projecting a linear reality outside of yourself, and the creator state of feeling: "I am infinite power. I am infinite abundance. I am Infinity itself." You become very attuned to the difference between these two modes of being. And you become convinced that you *can* stop taking your cue from circumstances. You understand that you can do that safely and with integrity. Why? Because that's how Creation works.

"Creation" means you are creating, right? So, why take the victim role of receiving? This is *creation;* this is not *receiving.* No one ever said, "all of Receiving." No, it's "all of Creation." Every single moment is a new creation, and you're generating it. You're adding to the expansion of The One exploring itself in new ways. That's why it's valuable. That's why it's in integrity with The One for you to overpower your reality with your preference. Your preference is your guidance to the most immediate, effortless way to become most fully yourself.

So keep practicing. Persist in seeing only your preference, and forget about appearances and circumstances. You only see what you place in front of you, only your own chosen frequency. You don't see what is beyond that because there is nothing beyond that. Remember, this is what you're doing already; I'm not telling you anything new. I'm just reminding you of what's happening all the time unconsciously. And as you keep practicing, you will start to feel it.

When you have nailed it, you will be in a state of abundance, a state of connection, the state of Infinity, the state of "I am the generator; I am not the receiver. I am the Creator of reality, not the beggar. I am here to create, not to beg or to ask." Ask and thou shalt receive? Yes, but you are asking *yourself* to give you something. So, start giving to yourself; it's more immediate.

At the same time, using questions creatively is one way you can tune into the frequency that represents what you want to give yourself. Questions are useful because they work as tuning forks—they tune you into a certain frequency. "Let's see, how would it feel to be like that? Oh, it would be like this." Then choose the frequency that your questions led you into. Your imagination responded to the questions and allowed you to tune into something; now choose that and make it all that you see. Prioritize this over everything and everyone else. Only see what you desire to see. Only be what you prefer to be. Only feel what you want to feel.

It's really safe to do this. You would be surprised at how safe it is. You won't turn into a murderer or a rapist or anything like that. In fact, you'll be surprised at how loving you will become. You'll be surprised how much of a father in Consciousness you will become, how much of a mother in Consciousness you will become. From the human point of view, it is a weird system; it seems counter-intuitive. But, when something seems counter-intuitive, it usually works. (That being said, if it really seems counter-intuitive, follow your intuition. Are you taking advice from me, or are you seeing only your preference? Don't listen to what I say, right?)

The only time it may get confusing is if you assume the victim seat. Nothing is confusing once you realize *you are generating everything*. You are generating the question. You are generating the confusion. You are generating the answer. *It's beautiful!*

*   *   *   *   *

Q&A

Question #1

Questioner: I've had a big shift here in the last hour. I created you to not be there while you were speaking the whole time. And I only heard you because that's what I preferred. At one point, I was watching your shadow on the wall and I preferred that. It all felt so easy, and I was able to absorb it and ignore it, and take in whatever was relevant.

So, I started thinking about my health, because I used to create this thing called "adrenal fatigue." Well, I used to create it up until an hour ago!

Bentinho: Good.

Q: Now I'm just creating ease. I can already feel myself becoming this thing called "health." So, I'm just going to keep doing that, and I know my health will return. I saw what I was creating—I used to do this thing called "seeking, and trying, and efforting"—and making life hard. You have taught me to impose ease and to relax; to be lighthearted and enjoy. This is my preference.

B: Good. See only that. Be only that. There is nothing outside of your preference field to wait for or to get permission from—nothing. *It's not there*. It's not that we ignore, really; it's that we remember that it was never there to begin with. And all we see is, "Hey, we are creating, we are creators, we are nothing else. We are not 99% creators and 1% receivers of an actual reality—we are 100% creators." So, thank you for taking up that Creator seat once again, instead of the victim seat. Be in the Creator seat—not the asker seat, not the beggar seat. Be the Giver, the Generator, the Creator, the Decider, the Chooser. This is empowerment.

Practice right now. Ignore this situation, ignore me, and see only what you want to see. Ask yourself, "What do I want to see? Oh, this is what I want to see, so this is what I'm feeling right now. This is what I'm seeing, this is what I'm exuding. And you will fill up with love so much that it may actually extend to other people inside of your own creation.

Question #2

Q: **Well, first I wanted to share my experience of this.** When I'm practicing this and forcing myself upon my creation, I feel my own energy so strongly, like it is coming out of my eyes and coming out of my whole body and filling the whole room!

B: Yes.

Q: And it's really intense! It's very strong and beautiful to do that.

The other thing that was really an interesting insight was when you said, "You've been doing this all along." I was thinking, "That's true—I have created this. I have created such a great life for myself, being here in Colorado, being in this community, having these teachings and all these friends. So, I've been doing a pretty good job so far. Or at least lately, anyway—it wasn't always this great!

Something else I noticed is that, when I feel the energy of my soul going outwards, I get what you say—that this is sort of dominating my reality. But to me, it's also like "giving." It's like totally giving my heart, my love, my whole self to my creation.

B: Yes, perfect. Thank you. Awesome!

Question #3

Q: So, this is my first experience generating you.

B: Oh, wow! Powerful, for a start.

Q: Every year, for the past several years, I have chosen a word to focus on. And the word I chose for this year was "receptivity." Hahaha!

B: What a beautiful generation!

Q: So, that's kind of been blown out of the water. Haha!

B: Good! Now understand that all qualities are valid qualities, right? So, I'm not saying the quality of receptivity is a bad quality. I'm saying the assumed state of mind that one is a receiver of reality is an illusion. You can be the generator, not the receiver, if that feels good to you. You can be the generator of the feeling of receptivity. There's a difference between that and just blindly assuming that you're at the receiving end of the stick of God. I'm talking about the state of the receiver, of being the receiver or the conceiver. I'm not talking about the quality of receptivity, which can be a very beautiful quality. Receptivity can be very Love-Light infused. And you can generate it, but just know that you are generating it.

What do you really want to feel? Why did you choose "receptivity" as your word, to begin with? What did you think it would lead you to?

Q: I thought it would lead me to what I wanted to create in my life. I thought I was somehow blocking myself. It actually feels more like the victim-y stuff you were talking about.

B: Sure, yeah. So, now you know you can generate what you wish to generate, without first having to generate being the receiver of what you wish to generate!

Q: Without having to first generate that I have blocks?

B: Yes, thank you. Exactly.

Q: Right! So, what I really want to experience is this feeling of… I'm just going to call it "charm."

B: Charm? I love that! Because you are very charming, to be honest. It's working.

Q: And it feels really good! It gets me excited to even think about it. Thank you.

B: It will work; it always does. What do we wish to generate? Because that's all we're doing anyway. So, let's generate what we *want* to generate—instead of what we don't want to generate and then ask questions about it, right? And then we call that "spiritual development!"

Can you see that? Can you see how you generated the illusory state of being a receiver? And that illusory state doesn't feel good, precisely because it's not true. Then we start asking questions—and we create religion, we create spirituality, we generate enlightenment, and we start thinking in terms of gurus, teachers, students, books, and all of that stuff. But all of that is only created because we first create the sense that we're separate, that we're limited, that we're at the receiving end of the generation of experiences. Realize that you can bypass all of that.

Q: Yeah—what I'm generating is joy, this vibrant happiness to be alive. And I see myself waking up in the morning, just so happy to be alive. And blessed. And connected—this feeling of deep connection to everyone else. I enjoy the pseudo-separateness, just to enhance that sense of love.

B: Thank you. That's beautiful. Isn't that gorgeous? He sees that he creates the illusion of separation so that he can experience a more intense type of love; he generates the two-ness of it. That is beautiful: "I create separation so that I can enjoy unity." That's exactly what The One's original thought was: "I want to experience myself, so I will create something other than myself—experiences, awareness, consciousness." Infinity is not conscious; it is not aware because it is infinite. Awareness is a finite concept. It is generated because *experiences* are required in order for The One to know itself in all of these different ways. So, it had the same thought as you!

Keep remembering to ignore that there is a circumstance happening. There is no circumstance happening; all you're witnessing is the intensity of your own Presence, colored with your own frequency of choice. That's all you ever experience. What frequency of choice are you infusing your infinite Presence with right now? And right now? And right now? It requires some new habituation to become proactive in this way. "Hey, wait a second... I can feel whatever I want to feel, I can generate whatever I want to generate. I can choose how I want to experience this moment. Who would have thought? I can actually choose how I wish to experience this moment!" You have to remind yourself over and over again so that you get out of the state of being a receiver, out of thinking, "This is just how reality is, and I can sort of feel good about it or sort of feel bad about it." No! Always ask, "What do I wish to generate right now?" And that becomes all that you see.

Question #4

Q: Umm...this feels funny to say. So let me just say it: I am sweet to me. And this is what I always wanted in the world.

B: Is that true? Are you seeing a group of people, or are you seeing sweetness? I am looking at all of you, but all I see is that *I* am a really sweet being. I don't have to actually see "you." I can look you in the eyes and see that I am a really sweet being, and the more present I become with my own chosen frequency, the more I actually get a sense of you—the more I notice your Higher Self, instead of just whatever I was thinking about you. So it's ironic, because again, it's counter-intuitive. You think, "Oh, I'm separating myself from other people because I'm not paying attention to them." For me, when I'm listening to someone, I'm hardly ever listening to them. Honestly, I'm just experiencing my own Presence. I'm experiencing what I desire to experience. And sure, the mouth and the body, they go, "Oh really? Awesome! Good for you, I am so happy for you! Nice! Epic!" But I'm *experiencing* what I desire to experience, and what happens is that I start to sense the person's energy opening up, and their energy starts to reflect that lightness and that presence and that permission to just be themselves.

When that matches up, there is true connection. But there can't be true connection when you feel obligated to listen to someone's separate story from your separate self. You need to give yourself permission to be and see only what you prefer to see, frequency-wise, in that moment. This gives the person permission to either match that or not, to rise up to that state of confidence and openness. And when they do, that's when lovemaking happens—"lovemaking" in any form, not just in the traditional form. Just love-making. That's when there's a generation of true connection, and that's the very first step of what it's truly like to be connected on a Higher Self level. It's sort of like the first conscious reflection of that, in what we could call "physical reality." So, you are sweet to yourself. That is beautiful. Feel just that. Does it feel good?

Q: It does. Right now, I feel a little frozen because I feel scared.

B: That's beautiful. How would you like to feel?

Q: I guess I would like to feel embraced and warm and that we're playing.

B: Beautiful. And simply talking about it already starts to generate it a little bit, you know. The fear can be there. Can you see that? The fear is actually part of the circumstances, like this table. This table does not indicate how I should feel about it. So, if I'm afraid of it, that doesn't mean I should feel afraid of it. I can actually feel really sweet about my own fear. Like the table, the fear is also circumstantial. You can see only that which you wish to see, whether fear arises or the frequency of your choice arises in the body.

The frequency is not in the body ultimately. The body can translate it into feelings, but you can see the frequency you wish to feel and see, regardless of how the body feels, regardless of how the mind acts up. Even the mind and the body are circumstances, as much as the plant over there is, or the Great Wall of China is. Beautiful! So, give me some more statements about what you desire. What do you prefer to see more of?

Q: The main thing was I am sweet to me, because that was what I always looked for out there, and I didn't see very much of it.

B: To be embraced, to be loved, to be sweet. Yes.

Q: The other one is that we are playing.

B: And aren't we?

Q: Yeah, we are. You are really good at it. I'm really good at it!

B: You are so fast. Yes, play! Play your heart out. There is nothing to fear. Fear, protection, and defense are related to the idea that there is an outside world. When you see that the outside world is generated by you—therefore, it must be made out of your own energy—then suddenly you feel, "Oh, wait… I am free to play! Nothing can ever harm me because it is whatever I say it is." Beautiful! "I am sweet to me"— that is gorgeous. That's a gorgeous frequency right there, "I am sweet to me." Beautiful. Thank you.

Question #5

Q: I am in love with feeling this absolutely flawless crystal-clear quality. It feels razor sharp. It's a sense of being absolutely, inseparably myself.

B: Yeah, wow! I can feel it, I can see. It's beautiful.

Q: Yeah, it is inseparability. And I think of congruency as well, but even that thought feels like it is two. But it's not; it's not two. It's just the unfolding and the sense of the story of "me" absolutely gone and no longer needed. It's the bliss of being absolutely totally here, and forever now on the edge of exciting, ever-expansive, unknown, exhilarating possibilities.

B: Yeah! Amen! Thank you.

So often we don't give ourselves permission to be in our own state of being, right? Especially around other people. It's such an automatic assumption that, because there are other people around, we should listen to them. But do you realize you could literally be at a party for two hours, talking to someone who is eating their heart out, telling you their story. And you could not hear a single word and just look around yourself, and that would absolutely be respectful. It is not known to our society, but your state of being is your own—always.

Question #6

Q: I am not able at this time to generate an explanation as to why the Creator started this whole thing in the first place. There is no lack in that being, so why would it need to know itself even further?

B: Do you mean Creation at large or creation in the form of you?

Q: The Creator—the Creator of All-That-Is. Why did it start to want to know itself? What provoked it?

B: Well, *you* tell *me*. Tune into it. Give yourself the answer. You can give it to yourself through me, eventually; that is one possible answer. But you can also give it to yourself through you. What do you think? What do you feel when you tune into that question? The question is not about you being the receiver of something; the question tunes you into the frequency where that answer is obvious. That is what questions are for—they tune you into an alternate frequency within which answers and solutions and creations are already present. So, why did the Infinite Being—which is already complete, which is not lacking anything, because it is infinite—why would it create experiences? You tell me, you tell you, me tell me, it tells it.

Q: I was hoping you were going to do it.
   Haha! I can't get past, "Uh, it was bored?"

B: Thank you. Well, there you go. Awesome.

Q: No, no… It does not compute; it does not compute. Access denied!

B: So, then what's the answer?

Q: I don't know!

B: Come on—you are that Creator. You started this whole thing and now you're asking me. Why did you start Creation, oh dear Creator? Why did you start creating? Why did you start generating an experience of yourself?

Q: Actually, to increase the capacity of love. The capacity of the fullness, the expansion and contraction... so it would be bigger, wider, fuller.

B: See—you can always find your own answers. Not that getting it from someone else is not an answer from yourself, too. Of course it is, but you don't always have time to be at a meeting or to read a book. You can accelerate the expansion of your knowledge, your download, your intuition, your intuitive way of responding to life. You can expand yourself by knowing, first of all, that you can come up with your own answers. And as soon as you start to trust the answers, even if they seem not entirely accurate, they start to become more accurate—because you trust them. "Oh, wait... I *did* get some kind of answer. OK, but now what about this aspect of it and that tiny sub-aspect of it?" More and more, it becomes a really complete and holistically accurate answer. As soon as you know and remember that you can choose to get your own answers, by no other means than through your own intention, that is very powerful. It has been a crucial part of my journey.

Quite early on, I accepted the fact that all the answers were inside of me. Otherwise, I wouldn't be here today, speaking to you as confidently as I do about things that I have not read in any books. Well, I read about certain things, but there were so many things that no one confirmed to me. I'm not waiting around for my father to agree with me. I'm not waiting around for Mooji to agree with me, or some other teacher. I am not waiting. If the answer comes through and it feels totally resonant, if it fits into everything I know, and it's logical (because Creation is logical), then it's like Bam! When you feel it, it makes sense and you *know*. The answer is right there, with no other requirement. If it feels true, that's all you need.

Question #7

Q: Why are you creating us?
B: Why am I creating you? Relevance. Why are you generating me, seemingly generating you?

Q: Because of love.

B: Well there you go. Yes. Ultimately, the reason for any creation is love. Perhaps not "love" as we generally know it, but love because there is only One Being, and it wants to know itself. That is what love is. The One Infinite Being wants to know itself. Love is self-love. Love is the One Being's own love for itself, for its potential, for its infinity, and for wanting that to be made manifest.

This love has many offspring; it has many facets. It has many distortions, which are all beautiful. But ultimately, love is the fact that there is only One Being, and it wants to know itself. That is its own love affair. It's like, "Hey, not only I-AM, but I-AM *and* I want to know that I-AM. I want to know that I exist." Infinity cannot know that *it is* without expressing itself and experiencing itself in form, in manifestation, in experience—using Awareness, the free agent, the first principle of Infinity. It generates all of this out of the love of knowing itself. Ultimately, that is the only love there is—The One wanting to know Itself.

This is what we are doing when we look into each others' eyes. This is such a beautiful symbol for The One to know itself—to look into another's eyes. That's one way for it to express itself; it is The One looking at itself. All of this creation is really The One looking at itself. You are that One that wants to know itself, and so you are generating this reality. This is just one of your many realities.

* * * * *

Guided Meditation

To watch or listen to this guided meditation visit:
bentinhomassaro.com/super-accelerated-living

Relax your body and your mind—as part of your creation. You can either keep your eyes closed, or keep them open—sort of gazing in a subtle relaxed state, not too focused on objects in your environment. Just relaxed.

And take a deep breath. Tap into the feeling—that core, fundamental, non-physical feeling at the heart of your being—the closest you can get to your True Self. Away from all distraction. Go deep, deep inside that core feeling, that core remembrance that you are the Creator of your life.

Dive into that feeling. It is totally present to you. When you do, you will find that the world disappears. It is reabsorbed into the space of "I AM the Generator of this dream. I-AM the Creator of my world. I-AM the Giver of realities. I-AM the Infinite One Creator."

Dive deep into that feeling and make it your world. Make it all there is for you. Make your frequency, your preference, your connection to yourself the only truth. Make the feeling "I-AM the Creator" your entire presence, your entire world, until everything else fades away and is reabsorbed back into its original form.

See, state, and feel only your heart's true preference. What do you, as the creator of your world, prefer? What do you choose? What do you desire? What do you long for? Give that to yourself. Give that to your world. Become consumed by it.

Remember, there is nothing but this. You have never not experienced your state of being. You have never not experienced your Creator seat. There has not been a single experience in your life where what you felt was not yourself, was not your own state.

You cannot escape your own Presence. You never have and you never will. So, why not color it with all the joy you can imagine—with all the love, with all the light you can conjure up—knowing that you are the Creator, knowing that you are the Generator, knowing that you are the Chooser of your state. It has always already been so. Now utilize it. Make it yours. Have fun! Have fun with it for the first time ever. Have fun with the way Creation is actually structured, with the way reality actually operates.

Choose your vibe. Paste it onto everything you see, bring it with you wherever you go. Taste, feel, smell, and experience only your preference, your creatorship, your value, your presence, your worthiness, your infinite nature. Experience it now, more so than you experience any physical stimuli. Experience your preference more than you experience these words. Experience your state of being, more than you experience your environment.

Your state is so powerful and all-consuming that it generates worlds and worlds and worlds, every single second, without your knowledge. As it becomes more conscious, you remember that you are a god (or a goddess, if you have that preference). This is yours: what you see is what you are. It is what you exude. It is what you choose. What you choose is what you see. What you feel is what you create. What you see is a reflection of what you are *being*.

Imagine the highest. Tune into the highest for you. Knowing that you are the creator of your reality, tune into the highest possible state for you, and make that your world. Make only that your world. Dive into it and force it upon your surroundings. Overwhelm your surroundings with the frequency of your choice, as if that is all that can potentially be.

There is no other choice but to express yourself by feeling your chosen frequency everywhere you look. For every interaction you have, feel only your preference. Make your preferred state of being all you see, all you decide, all you choose, all you believe in. And that's it. Your world ends with you. Your world ends with your preference. It begins and ends with your preference. This is how you consciously create. This is how you change and transform yourself, and the lives and connections all around you. This is how you give permission to yourself and others to remember that we are inseparable from the infinite One Creator that created All-That-Is.

Give this Infinite Being that we are the gift of knowing that it can be itself, that it can replicate and create itself in whatever way it sees fit. You need only your own permission. You are only waiting for your own permission to be a god once again—to overwhelm your creation with your newly chosen frequency, with your preferred state.

When the mind suggests that what you desire to see manifest is not happening, disregard that thought and return to the preference. Feel as if the preference is all there is. All you see is your preference. You don't see rejection. You don't see Yes and No. You don't care about the outside world, because there is no such thing. There never was. All you care about is your preference, the preferred state you wish to exude— the state you wish to manifest, the state you wish to impress upon your reality.

Over and over and over again, choose your preference over your circumstances. Choose your creation over the answers of other people. Choose to see only what you prefer, regardless of the results. Results don't matter to you because, either way, all you see and experience is your preference. So who needs results anyway? Be your preference...be your preference...be your preference.

In other words, be yourself. Be yourself. Everyone is waiting for it! Be one of the first to not wait for this anymore. Give others permission by your example. Do you want to help others? Then give yourself permission to be only your preference. This gives others permission to truly, for the first time, connect to spirit, connect to your spirit, connect to their spirit. This collective co-creation will then appear to become a happier place, as well.

Thank yourself for being awesome. Thank yourself for being epic. Thank yourself for being a god. Thank yourself for being God, for being the creator of your reality. You have a God-given gift to create—not to ask, not to beg—but to create, to generate, to decide, to choose, to put in place, to impress. You are here to impress upon the field of unconditional potential, unconditional love. You are not here to take or receive. You are here to give. You are here to shape.

Take your blueprint, which is your preference—your true desire, your true intuition, your true ins-piration—and see only that, feel only that, be only that. Execute upon only that. Speak only of that, and think only of that. If you do so, your life will become an epic testimony of the fact that you are God. Magic will become normal. Love, peace, and ease will be natural, effortless, and almost meaningless, because they are so present. They will be so effortlessly present that all you will be interested in is "What is the next most joyful thing to generate? What is the next most exciting, uplifting, empowering thing to generate—for myself and for the rest of my Self, the rest of my creation?"

Decide what the most exciting thing to generate is, and be that, see only that. Make it happen, no matter the responses you get. You are king of your reality. You are god of your world. Do not take no for an answer, do not take any answer to mean an answer. There are no answers. Do not take your cues from that which does not exist, which is circumstances. *Give* your cues. *Give* yourself.

Take a deep breath and feel powerful—because you are. Feel infinitely powerful, feel infinitely expanded and extended. You are everywhere all at once, moving at infinite speeds while remaining absolutely still. And thank yourself.

*   *   *   *   *

Part II:

How to Use Parallel Realities

People are stuck in mediocre or unsatisfying lives simply because they don't know the rules of the game. They have never learned how the universe really operates, mechanically or structurally. In this meeting, Bentinho first lays out the ground rules, the cosmic operating instructions (the driver's manual!). Then he explains how to practice and apply these rules in daily life—*for those who care enough to create an epic human experience.*

Some of you may be familiar with the idea of parallel realities. If you're not, it's simple enough—just *very different* from what you've been taught. Here are some of the basic points that are covered in this meeting.

- There is no such thing as linear time; time, structurally speaking, simply does not exist.

- Everything happens in the Now. All possible realities, past and future, and all unexplored realities (an infinite number of them)—all exist in the Now.

- The Now is not, as people typically imagine, a moment of rather brief duration in between past and future. The Now is timeless and transcendent to past, present, and future; it contains and transcends all three.

- Everything is static...EXCEPT consciousness. Consciousness has free will to move along the path of its choice within infinite static parallel possibilities—thus creating the experiential illusion of time.

- Since these are all happening in the Now, they are accessible to you from your Presence in the Now. That means you can jump timelines.

- You change your reality by changing your frequency, by increasing your vibration of excitement to match your preferred parallel reality.

*   *   *   *   *

"You're not stuck in this one life; you never have been. There are infinite parallel lives that look nothing like who you are today. My intention is to help you understand that you can become anything you desire to become. You can understand this principle to such an extent that six months from now you will not recognize yourself. Six months from now, or even sooner, if you truly understand this principle

and you start practicing what I'm sharing, you will not recognize yourself—I guarantee it.

*There are very clever tools and techniques and ways of seeing life that can allow your preferred reality to come through much faster. It's all about letting go of the resistance to the infinite possibilities that coexist as parallel realities. It is about understanding that this is how reality works; this is what is **actual.** This is not science fiction."*

-Bentinho Massaro

This meeting was streamed live on January 26, 2015 in Boulder, Colorado.

* * * * *

There is no linear time

The idea that there is linear time is an *agreement*. It is not an actual, physical, mechanical, energetic fact of the universe.

In every moment that you have an experience, you are quite literally experiencing an alternate reality in which *everything* has changed from the previous reality. The assumption is that things change within the *same* consistent linear reality, but this is not actually true. It's not that there is one consistent reality in which your molecules move around independently.

Every little change is a *complete change*, a complete shift of the total universe, not just bits of the universe. Every tiny motion, every movement, is actually within a completely different reality. This means there are countless different realities between my hand being over here and my hand being over there. Consciousness can configure, or view, those realities so seamlessly that it seems like it's one continuous reality, when in fact, I'm in one reality... and then in a different reality... and then in a different reality... each time I move my hand. There is a constant shifting of realities. That, in a nutshell, is the idea of parallel realities.

One very important phenomenon that comes with this understanding is that your sense of time becomes completely different. When you really understand the concept that I just described, linear time disappears for you—in the sense that you see it is an illusion, or a projection. You see that it's an agreement. The idea that there is linear time is an *agreement*. It's not an actual, physical, mechanical, energetic fact of the universe.

So, the idea of parallel realities brings with it the concept of non-linear time or, from another point of view, *timelessness*.

There is no experience outside of consciousness

Let's start with consciousness. You are conscious of my voice. You are conscious of your body sitting in a chair. Have you ever had an experience you were not conscious of? Have you ever experienced a reality without consciousness? No? Good!

Everything that has ever existed has appeared only to—or inside of—your consciousness. Just as in your dreams at night, even though your dream may seem "out there," as if you are visiting actual places, it is all happening *inside of your consciousness*. Reality is exactly like this. You have never experienced a reality outside of your own consciousness. Because there is none.

There is no reality outside of consciousness. There is no projection or experience outside of consciousness. Another way of saying this is: Nothing exists *independently* from consciousness. Objects and appearances do not have *Beingness*; they do not have existence of their own. They depend on con-sciousness, just as the experiences in your dreams at night do. It's not that objects and appearances in your dreams exist—that you go and visit them, and then you leave and they still exist. You *project* that you are going somewhere, but it's all happening inside absolutely still, motionless consciousness.

You are the center of the Universe. That is the basic idea, the basic realization you will have. I won't go too deeply into that now, because it's a whole different topic in and of itself. (I am assuming you have some familiarity with that.)

Even if you don't believe it's true for now, just assume that *Consciousness* is what you are. It's what is listening to my voice; it's what you can't escape, no matter how hard you try. You can run away from this meeting room and you will still be conscious. You can be hit by a car and you will still be conscious. You can talk to your mother and you will still be conscious (maybe a little less conscious, but you will still be conscious).

Consciousness is always here. Every experience you have meets inside of consciousness, inside of *you*. You can never change *you*, you can never leave *you*; you are inescapable. You as Consciousness, you as Awareness, you as the Witness, are inescapable. You as Sentience, you as Beingness, are inescapable.

Feel into that for a moment. Just stop thinking for 2 to 5 seconds. Give away all your thoughts and notice the space that remains—the clarity, the consciousness that is still here, the I-AM that still exists. The very obvious, overwhelming sense "I-exist" exists whether you're thinking or not thinking. But when you're not thinking, it becomes very clear that "I-exist" exists independently from everything that appears. *Regardless of what appears, you exist.*

Consciousness can never be escaped. It is the ground of all experiences, the meeting point of all experiences. In fact it is the center of the universe. So imagine that within this consciousness there is the availability of infinite possibilities, or infinite possible configurations of energy. Energy, which is one of the aspects of consciousness (Consciousness-Energy), can shape itself into whatever is possible.

On a universal, cosmic, infinite scale, everything that can ever exist *already exists.* Any possible configuration of energy that can ever be created already exists. But your individual experience is, obviously, not that vast. *Your individual experience is determined by where you shift your consciousness.* In this life, in this experience you are having right now, consciousness sets itself up in such a way that it constantly creates, or shifts into, a view of reality that looks very similar to the previous one, and then very similar to the previous one, and so on. It does this so that we can have the illusion of a linear timeline, but in fact, every single nanosecond is a 100% completely different, completely new reality. It is not *actually* new, because everything already exists, but it is *new to you* from your point of view, from your I-AM-Consciousness point of view.

The Movie Frames analogy

You change worlds every nanosecond. One way to imagine this is to use the analogy of a movie. You know that a movie consists of frames of images, and each frame is its own complete 100% reality. One frame has no structural relationship whatsoever to the next frame, even though they look very much alike. You could cut the reel of film, take one frame to China, and put another one in a rocket and send it to the moon.

The two frames have no relationship to each other whatsoever, even though they look so similar. For example, the only thing that has changed from one frame to the next might be the movement of a hand. In one frame, the actor´s hand is here; in the next frame his hand has moved slightly to the left. From a visual point of view, this is the only difference between the two images. However, from the point of view of the frame itself, all it knows is that *it is its own complete reality*, and that its molecules have no relationship to the molecules of the previous frame.

It's up to the *observer* to create the sense of linearity or "time"—based on this image, and then the next, and the next. You, as the observer of these images can say there is a "previous" and a "next" image. You can say, "First his hand was over here, and then it moved slightly left." But, from the perspective of the hand, nothing ever changed, because there is only one hand in that particular reality, or frame. The hand that is slightly more to the left is a 100% completely different reality that has no notion whatsoever of the other reality.

If you were to slow down a movie or "motion picture" (a picture in motion, and that's what life is, too) you could freeze a segment. What would that look like? What would one complete reality look like if you did not automatically shift into a new reality? It would look like everything was absolutely frozen. Hypothetically, you could keep your consciousness in one such frame—you could "pause" the process so that all you are aware of is one timeless total configuration of Universal Energy.

Every time *you* change (which is constantly), your reality changes. It's a constant reflection of who you *are*, a constant reflection of the frequency of your consciousness, the state of your consciousness, and the point of view of your consciousness. Right now, you're in a 100% completely different reality than 10 seconds ago—really even a nanosecond ago.

Time is malleable – Learn how to influence it through presence

So, this moment is a completely new reality… and this moment…and this moment. What does that do to the idea of time? It makes it malleable. It makes it yours. It makes it influence-able, instead of a static, projected, externalized phenomenon that you are somehow trapped within. "Time," as an actual linear idea, starts to fade away in your mind, in your consciousness. And when a belief system ceases in your mind, *all the limitations that came with that belief system also cease for your experience.*

The more fully you understand this, the more you will be able to influence time—and your reality. You will be able to more fully experience and understand how reality is structured, how it actually works. Once you see clearly how reality works, you can start to *consciously* and intentionally utilize consciousness—which is already and has always been the master of your universe—to generate the results you desire.

Every reality is completely timeless. Every potential one-moment experience, every individual complete snapshot of the Universe exists eternally—it has always already been there and it will always be there. That means your reality does not change; instead, *you* shift into different realities.

This is how you generate the experience of change, the experience of time. Time is just an experience; it's not a mechanical, structural fact. Can you see how time is *subjective*? Can you see how it's not objective? When you realize time is subjective, interesting things start to happen. We could call this "acceleration"—the acceleration of your understanding of who you are, of the power that you are, of the consciousness that you are. You will start to embody the power of consciousness more and more, so that you will be able to influence the reality you choose to experience next.

Reality consists of individual "snapshots" of time. One way to visualize this is to imagine a large floor that is absolutely empty, except for pictures--endless rows of pictures filling up the floor. If you start at the top-left corner of the floor, you see a picture of your birth, and if you go all the way to the bottom-right corner, you see the picture of your death. All the other pictures show everything between those two events.

Once you realize that this is the way reality operates, you can make changes in the pictures. You can make changes to your past or to your future. You can experience a different present. Why? Because you realize that the present is the key to experiencing time in the way you wish to experience it.

What is "the present"? If all the pictures already exist, if all possible potential configurations of energy already exist, then there is no time in that. There is no choice in that. There is no freedom in that. Freedom lies in the present; but what is the present moment if everything already exists? If the future already exists and the past already exists, then what is the present?

The present is you. You are the present. You are the Now. You—your consciousness—is Now. Is it not? Your consciousness is all that is ever going to be Now. The reality you are experiencing right now already existed 100 trillion years ago; this conversation already took place. In fact it's still happening. And tomorrow it will still be happening. That's because to Consciousness, on its most fundamental level (which again, is not relevant for most people to experience, although it's the truth) there is no time whatsoever.

In a sense, the Big Bang is the explosion that caused all possible realities that could ever potentially be created to be created in an instant, all at once.

Everything was created at once. You are not actually creating anything new in terms of a new configuration of energy. If you build a sand castle in a particular way, it may be beautiful. We could call it "art," but you're not creating something that did not exist before. What you're doing is generating a *new relationship* with the structure that already existed in your future, and which you have now made manifest in your Now. Again, what is the Now? *The Now is your consciousness.*

What does it mean to manifest your reality from this point of view? To manifest your reality simply means to shift your consciousness to a certain vibration that lets a specific movie frame, or slide, fall into the projector slot. You allow a different slide to be illuminated by the projector beam. Every time you change your state of being, you will see significant changes in the slides that fall into the slot of your projector—into your consciousness.

The slides already existed. Making one slide manifest Now and removing another one does not mean that the other one ceases to exist—because you cannot take anything away from Existence. You cannot take anything out of Existence, and similarly, you cannot place anything into Existence, because where would it come from? Everything that can ever exist already exists; nothing can be removed from Existence and nothing can be added to it. Everything you can come up with, everything you think you could add to Existence, was already thought of at the moment of the Big Bang and has already been created. (Note that the Big Bang is just a symbol.)

If you can't remove anything from Existence, this must include your past experiences. Yes! It includes your past, and all other possible past experiences you chose not to have—which are infinite in number. There are endless different pasts that belong to you, or could have belonged to you, and they all still exist. You can't take a potential reality, a potential manifestation of energy, away from the Universe; you just can´t do that.

Because, *structurally speaking*, there is no time. Nothing new is ever created. Everything that can exist already exists, and will always exist.

Raise your 'Vibrational Attitude' to empower your life

Realizing these laws, your sense of time starts to become a little warpy, a little weird, because it removes all human perspective—everything you have been used to. But it opens you up to a much more empowered way of living, *a more conscious and more divine way of living,* and it allows you to influence what we call the "experience of time." Understanding these laws allows you to change the frequency of your consciousness, of your light, of your Now, of the present moment. We could call this frequency your "vibrational attitude."

Very briefly, your vibrational attitude is how you view yourself in any given moment. And *how you view yourself determines the way you experience life;* it determines your state of being. Your vibrational attitude is what you are constantly emitting—the energy or frequency of your being, the state of your consciousness.

You always have a vibrational attitude. That's why you generate a particular "slide" out of the field of All-That-Is to fall into your particular slot of I-AM-Consciousness. Your view of reality is now a particular slide because you were vibrating at the speed of consciousness of that slide. And *what you perceive always matches your frequency.*

In that sense, physical reality is like a mirror. It does not actually do anything to you; all it ever does is reflect you. All the time. All the time! It's constantly mirroring your state of being, your vibrational attitude, your consciousness. In this way, your particular configuration of consciousness turns into a particular configuration of experience within "physical reality."

So, how do you more consciously shift into an alternate universe, into a parallel reality?

First, remember: *You are already shifting right now.* Otherwise, you would not get from the first word of this sentence to the last word. You would be perpetually stuck at the first word. So you're creating your reality all of the time—shifting from one configuration of energy to another configuration of the universe. You're doing this constantly, on automatic pilot, *unconsciously.* It's great! It's fantastic! It allows you to be the "victim" of your creation, so that you can have the subjective experience of the illusion of time—the illusion of a particular personal theme that goes from A to Z.

But you're not stuck in this one life; you never have been. There are infinite parallel lives that look very similar to each other. And there are infinite parallel lives that look nothing like who you are today. My intention is to help you understand that *you can become anything you desire to become.* You are not stuck in the conditioned reality that you have been given by your previous choices and your previous creations.

You can understand this principle to such an extent that six months from now you will not recognize yourself—even if this is the first time you're hearing about this principle. Six months from now, or even sooner, if you truly understand this principle and you start practicing what I'm sharing, you will not recognize yourself—I guarantee it. You will look at pictures or you will see a video of yourself, and you will think, "Who is that guy? Who is that person? What does he have to say?"

You will start to forget things—which is a good thing by the way, because it allows more space for new things. You don't totally forget things: if someone brings up a memory, you can usually still tap into it—depending on how distant that reality is to your present frequency of being. But in general, you become more "slippery." You become more empty, more free, more available for your present Now to become whatever you want.

You stop living in the illusion of a linear reality with a given past and a given future. You start waking up to the fact that there is no time; that there is only Now—and that you can insert into the field of Now whatever **vibratory pattern** you wish to insert, whatever **vibrational attitude** you wish to carry. As you do this, you will see that reality warps around you, not the other way around. You are, in that sense, a god. You are, in that sense, a creator. You are not a victim. You are not a slave. You are not a beggar. *You have created this reality.*

I am not teaching you anything new. If you didn't already know how to do this—automatically—you wouldn't be able to follow this conversation. You would be stuck in time. But, instead, you are effortlessly generating a consensus parallel reality... and another consensus parallel reality... and another. We are moving together because our alignment and our vibrations are similar enough to where we can generate the illusion of a consensus reality that moves from the start of this meeting to the end of it, "over time."

The whole time this is happening, you are Now. You are projecting different images into the Now...again and again and again into the Now. You are choosing your images out of a field of infinite, parallel, probable realities. In another reality you are doing something else right now, but you chose this particular reality because it's relevant to you.

I'm not saying you are doing this with your "conscious brain self." You *can* participate and co-create more and more with your brain self (your person consciousness), but for most people this ability has been given away completely to their Higher Self, to their Higher Consciousness.

Consciousness has infinite levels, and you are experiencing yourself at the level you assume yourself to be at. If you assume yourself to be at a very, very high level of consciousness, you will start to actually become that level of consciousness. You will be able to influence your particular timeline—not time, which doesn't exist—but *your timeline*. You will be able to influence the illusion of a timeline that you generate by going from this picture to that picture to that picture... and so on. Your particular timeline is based on each picture or slide you choose because it matches your vibratory attitude.

Increase your 'Perceptual Frequency' for super-fast learning

Your past has no structural relationship to your present. The reality of five seconds ago has no relationship to the reality of this second. If I move my hand, my hand is not over here due to the fact that it came from over there. My hand over there is always going to be over there. *And* my hand here is always going to be here. It never moved. It was never *on its way* from there to here. I shifted my consciousness to the reality in which my hand is timelessly over there, and then I shifted it to the reality in which it is timelessly over here!

You could call this the "flickering on and off of reality." Ancient yogis and rishis have said the same thing—that the Universe turns on and off in terms of Consciousness. It turns on and off all the time really quickly--like a flickering light, but it happens so fast that we don't perceive it.

In any moment, one potential configuration of energy becomes active; in the very next nanosecond another potential reality becomes active. Poof... poof... poof. Imagine flicking the light switch in your room on and off incredibly quickly, to the point where all you see is continuous light. But continuous light is not what's happening. With certain types of light, where the frequency of flickering is low, you get a sense of the discontinuity in the light (you can even get a headache from it). With old television sets, for example, you can see that half of the time there is no light at all. *Just as half of the time—in Creation—there is no experience, no reality at all!*

Similarly, if you increase your perceptual frequency, you will begin to see through the illusion of the flickering in and out of your Higher Self´s creation. You can increase your perceptual frequency (the vibratory state of your Now), which is felt as happiness, joy, excitement, bliss, ecstasy, inspiration, creativity, and feeling like you are on top of life. Anything that gives you a great sense of joy aids you in increasing your vibrational attitude, or vibrational state. When your vibrational attitude increases, your position on the ladder of infinite levels of consciousness goes up and up and up!

Each step you take on the ladder of infinite levels of consciousness—every time you increase your vibration, every time you know yourself to be more God and less victim, more creator and less slave, more on top of life and less underneath some kind of heavy piano—you increase the frequency of your consciousness to a higher level. This new level of consciousness already existed; it was already operational. You simply weren't aware of it from your point of I-AM, from your sense of identification of who you are.

Every time you increase your frequency you see a new reality, and you *gain access to more and more of your innate power to influence your reality.* As long as you assume yourself to be the victim, you will only get "victim power," which is very limited. Higher Consciousness is intelligent: it will never give full creation power to the victim, because it would destroy the Universe, in a sense. It would go mad. It would go crazy.

If you increase your frequency to the God level that you already are, you will see some real changes in your life and in your ability to positively affect the course of your timeline. You will extract more benefit from the experiences you have already generated for yourself and increase the speed at which you move through your lifetime's theme of exploring a certain idea. And that is why you are here—to explore, to express, to become something, to share, to learn.

The more you assume yourself to be the victim of creation, the more static you will be—like ice. As you increase your frequency, it's like the molecules start heating up—they start dancing in the ice. The ice starts to melt into water, which is malleable. Similarly, when you increase your frequency, your molecules start dancing up and down with joy, with excitement, with passion, with knowing you are God—the creator of your reality and the chooser of your universe. They dance with knowing you are the Eternal Now—which is in total control of its next picture. You become more and more empowered to make changes, and finally, you turn into "steam." Steam represents non-physical consciousness, which is a much fuller remembrance of who you actually are and what you're here to do. And then you can move faster... faster... faster!

Ice cannot move fast. Have you ever seen a glacier move? It's pretty slow. Have you ever seen steam move? It's pretty fast and it can go anywhere. You, similarly, can start to move really fast. You can learn from lessons more quickly because you gain access to Higher Intelligence, to a higher form of reasoning. Your mental body becomes the higher mental body. You start to understand and see things from a higher, grander perspective.

For example, in assessing a scenario involving a group of people in a certain emotional dynamic, in an instant you can know what's going on. You don't have to figure it out or think it through. In an instant you know what's happening, so you can move on to the solution. You ask yourself, "How should I behave right now to most positively accommodate the dynamics among these people?" And you know the answer!

So, you learn super-fast. You act super-fast, and in empowering and beneficial ways. You actually become *intelligent*, as we humans are supposed to be. You become less and less like a sheep, and more and more like a lion—an intelligent lion. You are no longer helpless; you are actually *creating*--being of benefit to yourself and everyone else. You're no longer reacting unconsciously—being slapped around by your thoughts and emotions, not knowing who you are or what you're here for, and therefore sending out to the Universe all kinds of mixed ideas and frequencies. This is all fine and perfect, of course, and there's no blame or judgement, but it is helpful to observe and become aware of your unconscious behavior—to let it motivate you to say "No" to that mode of being.

Or, do you not even care?

Everything depends on how much you care about your existence! If you don't care very much, that's fine, and you can keep being sheep-like and feeling like a victim. However, if you care about being alive, if you're excited about the potential that this incarnation offers you, then you'll start thinking. You'll ask questions and look into teachings such as these. Then, when a little brat like me tells you that maybe there's a higher step you can take for yourself, you take it. *You fucking take it!* Because you *care* about your life! Because you care about not going through your life unconsciously with the biases you have been taught by society—biases about what is moral, what is not moral, what your daddy taught you, what your mommy taught you, the fear of rejection, the seeking of love. And you start acting *consciously*. You take control of your own vibratory state. And when you do that, life becomes exciting and fun!

How fun was it, in your old life, to wake up every day with a paintbrush placed in your hand, but you're not controlling the brush? You are drawn to your canvas, but somebody else is painting with your hand! And you're forced to see this all day until you go to bed. You don't like the painting. You think, "Who the fuck is this artist? He can't paint shit! But, oh well... I don't know who I am, so fuck it. I don't care about my life; I'll just go sit on the couch." How fun is that? Is that fun?

Are you enjoying what you see—that which you *pretend* you're not creating? The invisible hand holding the paintbrush is *your* hand. You are painting, but you don't realize that you have the power to create whatever you want. You can suddenly stop the paintbrush, pick a different color, and paint all over your previous creation.

Now, how fun would it be to wake up every day and choose whether or not you *feel like* painting? If you choose to paint that day, you pick up the paintbrush you prefer—the one that feels like it suits your mood—and then you start dipping into the colors that attract you and paint what pleases and fascinates you. *And* you can take a break whenever you want to! You don't have to look at the painting all day. You can go have some food; you can call your mum if you want to, and get back to your painting later whenever you feel like it.

Now, if the canvas is your life, and if that's really true (and *it is true*, whether or not you believe it), what I'm saying is that you can actually generate a reality you desire—a reality of your preference, of your alignment, of your truth, of your theme.

One thing that's very crucial to understand is that you are constantly painting your life; *you are constantly sending out a message.* I know that sounds sort of New Age-y, but it's true. You are constantly sending out messages. To whom or to what? To yourself, to your creation, to the mirror that reflects you. You are constantly shaping the image in the mirror that reflects you. So, you need to be a little bit mindful of what you're sending out! Check in with yourself— what are you thinking right now?

You would be surprised how unconscious people are of what they're thinking on a daily basis. Maybe you don't notice now, but as you start to increase your level of consciousness, you begin to see that everyone is sheep-like. They have no idea what they're thinking. They have no idea why they're saying things. There is no clarity. There is no decision in any single one of their random choices. And then they wonder why their lives seem so incoherent!

Well, their lives are incoherent because that's what they're creating. They're sending out the message, "I don't care about my life. You create it for me." And by "you" they mean other people, social conditioning. So, people basically give away all their power to parents, friends, childhood teachers, the people on television, the advertisements they see. They give away their power to all those outside influences. And they're sending out the message, "I don't care about my life. I don't care about being happy. I don't care about what I came here for; this is a waste of energy anyway. You guys go right ahead—create my life for me! I'll just watch..." This is not a recipe for happiness, let me tell you that! It is not!

But there is *a recipe for happiness.* Otherwise, I would not be sharing this; I would just be doing the same thing everyone else is doing. I am sharing this with you because there is a recipe. There is a solution to the unconscious madness, to the rambling that you are not even aware of. The solution is to become aware of the madness and to start intentionally choosing your vibration, choosing your state of being, choosing what you believe in. Always choose where your attention goes, because where your attention goes, that's where your energy will flow.

The reason you have let yourself drift on "random automatic pilot" is because you assume you have no power. So you just let things ramble on. Because of this, what you experience is a very mixed bag of things, a life that seems completely random, and also completely taken care of for you, but not in a positive way. It's like you are taken care of in the sense that you have no free will, that everything "just happens." Perhaps you have free will in terms of whether you picked the green apple or the red apple. But if you are unconscious of even that choice, then you will pick the one your automatic pilot says you will pick.

Free will is a given of the Universe, but it's dependent upon your level of consciousness as to how much access to your original free will you will regain. If you are acting unconsciously and don't care much about your life, then you will create the illusion that you lack free will.

So you *do* care? Then here's how to practice

If you want to make your choices conscious, you must start practicing. I know that might sound boring or tedious, but it's actually very practical; it's actually very effective. Here's the good thing: you start to see results immediately. This gives you feedback in a positive way, which then gives you confidence— leading to transformation and confirmation. And you can continue to do this and expand upon this until you reach levels you can't even imagine yet.

You start to understand and see and create at speeds you don't believe possible from your present vibratory state of consciousness. You don't believe it's possible because you cannot yet create like this from your present vibratory state of consciousness. But by the time you're in the vibratory state of consciousness I'm talking about, it will be like breathing to you. It will be as normal as it is for you to choose the red apple or the green apple. Things you call "magic" from your current point of view will be "normal" in the next stage of life. Things will speed up. Your creation will reflect your true desires more and more and more.

But this requires that you remain alert; you must remain mindful about what you're telling your universe. What are you telling your universe right now? What are you believing in? What level are you vibrating at? Can you become aware of that right now? Just tune into yourself. What assumptions are you under right now?

You are always under certain assumptions—for example, that gravity exists. Oh, you didn't notice that? It's something that you have assumed. That's why it's an "assumption" and why it's unconscious.

Gravity was created for you so you can walk on planet Earth without flying off. So, it's helpful! It's relevant. Nevertheless, it is an assumption. It's part of your unconscious consciousness, created out of an unconscious agreement. This is just one example to show you how you assume countless of things in any given moment. I do as well. We all assume a great many things at any given moment, things we are unconscious of. And that's quite alright, because many of these assumptions serve us. But many of them *do not* serve us anymore, and it's no longer relevant for them to remain unconscious. They can now be transformed, made conscious, and *chosen* according to your preference.

So, make yourself more aware of what you're sending out right now. What is the message you're putting out? What does your state of being feel like? Do you feel happy? Abundant? Are you looking forward to the next slide image? Or are you sort of like, "Mehhh…"? Because if it's "Mehhh," guess what the next image be like?

But, if you change your state of being, the next image will look a little brighter, and the next one after that even brighter. That will give you confirmation of the practice, and you'll become more confident, because now you *believe* you're an infinite creature with infinite potential. This is a very empowering belief because it's in alignment with your Higher Self. It will encourage you to continue going higher—towards the Higher Self vibratory state. More happiness ensues. More power to create ensues, and the reflections in your reality confirm your progress. You expand; you become more confident that you are not a victim. In fact, you realize that you're not even a physical creature. *You realize that you are actually a consciousness with a state of being, and that's it.*

The body is part of the image you put in front of your eyes. You are not the body walking around in an actual world. The body came with the world you created. When you draw a picture on a canvas—a little guy with two legs and two arms, a little head—are you that little guy, or is he part of the world you created? Is he, in fact, inseparable from the larger canvas, from everything that surrounds him? When you go to sleep and dream you have a body, do you actually become that body? Or are you dreaming a body into existence that is inseparable from the environment that you are also dreaming into existence?

If you are ever confused about how physical reality works, reference your dreams. Physical reality works exactly like dreams. *Exactly.* You are dreaming your body into existence right now. And it's not the same body it was half a second ago. It is a 100% different body every moment because it's a 100% different universe and it comes with a different package. But you are not the package; you are the consciousness that chooses to be *aware* of a certain package with a certain reality.

Just as you are not your body, you are also not your personality. Can you be free from your own personality? Yes! You are free from it all the time. *You are consciousness with a state of being—and that's it!* There is no personality in that. Personality is a choice; it's like a coat you wear. Like the body, it's *part* of the world you create. It's another snap shot. One day you can be this personality; the next day you can be that personality—whatever suits the moment, whatever suits your mood, whatever is genuine for you in that moment.

You can express yourself through these means and become that personality with that body in that world and enjoy yourself in that creation, *until you feel a calling to consciously recreate yourself, to take a step back.* You pause for 2 to 5 seconds and take a deep breath. You recognize that you are Consciousness! You change your frequency and choose another image— thereby altering your timeline. Suddenly, instead of the timeline moving in a straight line, it moves like a zig-zag, going somewhere else. (Remember, you're always already in a parallel reality, so it's flawed to say "you shifted into an alternate reality," because you do this all the time.)

The trajectory you were seemingly following now drastically changes. It changes because you made a significant change in your identity, in your understanding of yourself, in your desire for yourself. It jarred your reality; it jarred you—your state of being, your personality, even your body. And now you're taking a different path. You're going in a different direction. To be more accurate, there is not actually a "direction"—there are infinite options available that are always already existing. You could say there are infinite directions. But as far as your experience goes, it's as if your timeline changed. You jumped up a few frequencies, and the song you are now playing, the reality you are creating, is different.

Don't take your cue from your circumstances

So, what are the rules of this new game? How do you do this stuff? *By changing your state of being, regardless of your circumstances.* Very important point: *regardless of your circumstances.*

Did you know you can feel however you want to feel, regardless of what appears in front of your eyes?

Someone could be flipping you off, and you could be absolutely happy about it or you could be absolutely distraught about it—it's up to you. If you choose to be offended, the next image will not be pretty; it could be a punch in the face. But if you choose to be happy about it regardless, that person may still punch you in the face, but your experience of that will be different. And the picture after that is guaranteed to be much more in alignment with who you truly are, because you stood the test of your circumstances. You stayed true to your new state of being, regardless of what occurred in your visual perception of energy. Stay true to your desired state of being. *Make it conscious— don't let circumstances run your life.*

Take a look right now at how strongly you believe that circumstances are real. Notice how many assumptions you have about circumstances being solid; these assumptions are all generating your reality. They cohesively create the illusion that reality is solid, and that external circumstances must be taken into consideration. These thoughts create your reality.

It may seem a bit hard to change, but the more awareness you bring into your experience, the more you can change your thoughts, your consciousness, your attention, your vibratory state. And suddenly, you will notice that you *can* generate alternate realities.

If you don't like the way things look—change your reality! *Why have you not done this before? Because you didn't know it was possible.* After all, what have we always been taught? To always refer back to "what-is." *This is a very bad habit; a very, very bad habit!* Parents and teachers told us, "Always refer to 'reality' and consider your circumstances. If you're confused about life, just get real. Get really real." And what is real? Taxes, mortgage, marriage, kids, responsibilities, putting food on the table. Will referencing these things make you happy? No. Hell no! It will make you depressed and crazy—so crazy, in fact, that you will believe your craziness is reality. Now, *that's* crazy. I think people call that "delusion."

So, choose your delusion wisely, because it will appear real to you. You can intentionally choose your delusion; you can choose your preferred reality and your state of consciousness. Every time you reference what-is, your current manifestation becomes the container for the next set of thoughts you'll have, for the next set of beliefs, for the next set of intentions. So by referencing your current reality, you will always generate a reality, a container, a manifestation, that looks like the previous one...and the previous one and the previous one. You will still be shifting through billions of parallel realities, but they will all be of a similar vibratory pattern, of a similar density of being. They won't look very different, and they definitely won't reflect more love and light back to you. That's why I always say, "Don't take your cue from circumstances—ever!"

This is what happens. People say, "Okay, what do I want? Well, this is what I have now. This is what I have now, so what can I do with that?" Very, very bad habit! It's the wrong way of thinking. Instead you should say, "This is what I have now; this is what is real right now... So fuck all that—I want something completely different!" Imagine that. Tune into that and it will become reality.

Imagination is your most powerful tool. It *is* Consciousness; *imagination is Consciousness*. It is real. You cannot imagine anything that is not already present inside of Existence. You cannot imagine anything that does not already exist. So, whenever you imagine something, *it exists*. It is just waiting for you. Where? Not even half a centimeter away. It's right there within the point of your consciousness that is *the meeting point of all of Creation*. It is the center of the universe and of all universes that coexist with it. There is no distance between this reality and that reality, between $10 and $10,000, between a partner and no partner. There is no difference between those realities; there is no distance. They coexist within the same zero-point, within the same singularity of Consciousness.

All that's needed to shift between them is a different vibration—and your preferred reality will start to manifest itself for you. And it will happen in terms that make sense to you, meaning most likely it will happen in a logical way. And you don't have to worry about that, it will just do that for you. Suddenly, this person shows up with a spare ticket to a concert you were just imagining going to. So now you go, "Oh...wait a second. Did I create that? Or was it just a coincidence? Did that person *just happen* to walk into the room with a spare ticket?"

You will make your manifestations logical and plausible to yourself by inserting things into your reality, one sequence at a time. One sequence at a time because we are conditioned to believe there is linear time: this comes first, and then that. You can't just jump from here to there! So, when you imagine things you want, you will also generate the sense of some time lag required. And this is great because you can learn from it; you can express different things in that gap of time.

The way to close that gap faster is to realize that Reality Z is as far from Reality A as Reality B is from Reality A. Why? Because one picture has nothing to do with another picture. One reality has nothing to do with the next moment's reality. *There is no structural causality anywhere.* Knowing this, your mind can start to see how reality works, and once you *see* how reality works, you start to *believe* that's how it works. Once you *believe* that's how it works, then the way a new manifestation comes to you can be far more flexible—because you're no longer as rigid in believing that things have to take a long time to manifest.

Reality will continue to appear to you in a way that's plausible to you. It must always honor your belief system and your level of free will. However, there are very clever tools and techniques and ways of seeing life that can allow that reality to come through much faster. It's all about letting go of the resistance to the infinite possibilities that coexist as parallel realities. It's about understanding that this is how reality works; this is what is *actual*. *This is not science fiction; this is fact.*

So shift your vibration! Decide what you desire next. Do *not* take your cue for what's possible based on what you see. Do *not* take your cue from your present container, because it's just a reflection of what you thought *before*.

What do you wish to create? When you think about this question, you must detach yourself from feeling tied to your present physical manifestation—the slide that's in front of your consciousness right now. Realize that you are consciousness—not the slide. The picture is your *creation*, not your consciousness. Realize that your consciousness has the ability to change the picture, to shift into a parallel reality *intentionally*. Realize this and set your intention. Know—or remember—that you want to be someone in a certain way, that you want to feel a certain way, and that *something is relevant for you that you've always kept small and suppressed*. What is it? Who are you really?

Who was your favorite superhero?

Who were you as a kid? *Who did you know you were?* Who was your favorite superhero? Your superhero is closer to who you really are than the person you've become. Minus Superman, obviously—since that's who I am! Actually, Superman is closer to the vibration I truly am than whoever I would have been, had I believed in all the nonsense other people told me.

Who is your inspiration? Everyone who inspires you shows you more of who you truly are. So, think of a few people—whether they are fictional characters or real people. (Both are the same thing because everything coexists and is equally valid in the eyes of consciousness.) What kind of people, or what kind of achievements are you inspired by? What do you look up to, in a good way? Who are your icons? Your answers will tell you who you are; at least a portion of who you are is reflected in them. They are reminders on your path, given to you by your Higher Self to inspire you to go in similar directions, to embody similar energies, and to emulate similar principles. Seek to match the vibratory state that these icons represent for you. Desire is your guiding compass.

Desire. Passion. *Life is passion.* You can understand this in a very distorted way, as most people do unconsciously. Or, you can take that same passion, or power, and flip it upside down in an instant. You can start using that power, that passion, to create your life in a way that actually works for you, in a way that's actually in alignment with what you came here to become and to express yourself as. So, make that shift in allegiance. Take back your power, and use it in a way that serves you.

Let go of all negative beliefs and all negative thoughts. Ease yourself into knowing there are infinite possibilities and infinite abundance. Believe in yourself. This is very important—more important than anything else, really. *Believe in yourself.* Believe in the True Self you know you are. Give it a voice. Give it a path. *Give it manifestation.*

*   *   *   *   *

Q&A

Question #1

Questioner: While we are in superman mode.... I'm creating that you are training a bunch of supermen and superwomen to dismantle nuclear weapons. We're on a planet with 50,000 or so little bombs that are nuclear. A group of people with screw drivers and maybe a wrench or two could take apart all these bombs in about two weeks.

So the question is: since physically we could do that with no problem, **what's the best way to work with government powers** to create a situation in which they would actually pay us to do that? That would be more fun than being put in jail. I would like to have more fun in my life, since all things are equally possible.

Bentinho: Dismantling nuclear bombs? What's your question?

Q: How do we change our consciousness so we actually believe that I'm not just a crazy man?

B: I'm not convinced you're not! We're all crazy. That's how we can all have our own reality, you see. We are all completely delusional, so I completely agree with your statement.

Q: I'm just asking how do we spread this consciousness? There's a government that I have to ask permission from in order to dismantle their bombs.

B: No, you don't. They are a reflection of you.

Own your government! It's your reality. There are infinite realities, and in some, the government is externalized as a creature of power that has power over the inhabitants. Nothing is further from the truth. There are other realities where that illusion disappears and the government starts to reflect the understanding of the collective. The thing to understand is that the government is us. It is us making our choices.

Understand that the government is not to blame for any single thing. Nor are its shadow operations, nor are the Illuminati, and so on. No one is to blame for anything. You know why they are seemingly in control? It's because we're lazy. We're lazy motherfuckers. We're vibrationally lazy. We're like, "Oh yeah, I don't care about my life."

Of course, someone has to take care of things. But we're not doing it. We're not choosing to be of the vibratory state where we are in control of our lives. By default, we are choosing to give away our power.

And then we complain about "the powers that be." Well, then take care of it yourself! Become who you really are. Start taking charge. Start inventing things to clean up the planet. Invent new monetary systems. Create groups. Create conscious vibrations.

If you wait for what happens to you, what you generate is external powers, which are still created out of your own Higher Self energy. They are just appearances, reflections of your own conscious energy, but you will make it look as if they are separate beings that have power over you. This only happens because you give it away, because you're waiting for your life to change. "If only they would change this, then I could be happy, then I could have what I want."

Stop waiting! When we as a collective stop waiting, the government will disappear completely. This doesn't mean there won't be any councils or things like that, but it will be completely different. It will be like a group of wise men and women representing humanity, transparently so, as actual representations of the collective consciousness. They will not be separate or segregated; there will be no secrets.

Speaking of secrets... I completely agree with the government that secrets must be kept from the public, although not ultimately. Why? Because you're not ready. You're not fucking ready. (Sorry for the language, but I am passionate.) You're not ready, okay? Ultimately, you will be ready, but right now, you're still taking on the sheep mentality.

The Universe is an exact match to us as a collective. It's a match to you as an individual, as well, because you choose the collective you are a part of, based on the individual you are. As long as you give away your power, as long as you feel like a victim, as long as you feel like you have no control over your life, you will always generate the exact reflection of that, out of your own energy—an externalized reflection. Then you blame the externalization, which is your own creation and your own choice, although forgotten.

Clearly, you're not ready to hear these secrets because they're not yet fully disclosed. The disclosure is happening gradually, yet more and more rapidly. Eventually, there will be a completely transparent governmental concept, until even that is no longer necessary, and even that will change. It will be a reflection of your readiness to embrace things you didn't know existed before, and your willingness to embody and integrate it in a powerful way, instead of in a scared and victimized way.

There are many things the government could disclose to you, but you're not ready for it. In that sense, I agree with keeping them as secrets, but only because keeping them secret is an exact reflection of you. This should inspire you to raise your level of frequency. Take responsibility for who you are. Feel that you're in control. Know that you are the Creator of the Universe. Then, there will be no need for secrets; you will be ready.

Question #2

Q: What is the most powerful practice?

B: The most powerful practice is out of reach for most people. But I will share it: *To know that it is done.* When we *know* something, it is fact, it is reality, and that becomes our universe. As soon as there is total knowingness, it will be reflected in your behavior, in your belief system, in your energy field, in your personality, in your actions, in your physical circumstantial reality, in your finances, in your relationships—everywhere.

Basically, everything you see, feel, and experience today is based on the level of knowingness you have, which is your state of being, your vibration. The most powerful technique is not really a technique; it is just a doing, it is an immediacy. It's like, "How do you move your arm?" You just do it. You just know it is done. You don't need any other "permission slips" in order to get to where you want to be.

However, for most people, in order to feel they have actually shifted knowingness, they need some time (which of course, does not exist); they need some permission symbols or practices. They need some experience of going through different types of frequencies and then feeling, "Oh wow! Maybe this is actually possible! OK, let me explore it, let me practice it. Oh hey… I see a reflection of it. Wow! It looks as if this is actually possible!" and so on. Then, at some point, they arrive at a higher level of knowingness.

The most powerful way to create your life the way you want it is to simply *know that it has already happened*, that it is true, that it is already so. If you can immediately shift your knowingness, then you no longer need any intermediate, in-between steps.

However, you do need some experience; you need to gain confidence in the fact that you *are* the creator of your reality. I'm not saying it's impossible to do it immediately, but it has been my experience that some practice and confirmation is necessary for most people—including myself. There are billions of choices I could not make starting right now, because I would need permission symbols in order to believe these things could be generated right away.

You always proceed from the point where you're at, based on the changing of your belief systems and on the practice and confirmations you get about the way reality works. This accelerates exponentially, meaning that, two days from now, I will be able to generate more than I can today. The degree to which I'll be able to create in two days will be a greater difference than the difference between two days ago and today. It's exponential.

You gradually become more confident in this knowingness. And it's an endless journey—both in this life and beyond this life. The empowerment journey is all about shifting your vibratory level, which is *what you know to be true*. So ideally, ultimately (for certain things at least), you can simply shift. You can know absolutely; you can absolutely know.

There's a difference between thinking and believing, and there's a difference between believing and knowing. Knowing is the most powerful. If you can go straight to the knowing aspect—knowing that something is done—then it is done. Because knowingness creates the reality you are in, so it becomes physical immediately.

Placing your desired future into your past

One fun technique that is actually quite powerful is to place something you desire to happen in the future, into your *past*. So, imagine something that resonates for you, something you desire. Normally, we create a distance between now and a desired future, which then creates the sense of lack, which then creates the *feeling* of lack. The feeling of lack then generates the lack of that reality, because what you are putting out is not "I have this" or "I am this," but "I don't have this" and "I'm not this."

Sometimes the seeing of what you desire, the imagining of it—tuning into your heart's reality, your true reality—can generate an even greater dis-satisfaction, because many people have learned to focus on lack. So, one crucial aspect of this is to diminish how much you focus on lack. Start focusing on abundance, regardless of how real or delusional it may seem to you. You must focus on the abundance of every moment. If you do, you will accelerate.

In terms of visualization technique, you can then take whatever it is you imagine is not here yet and *place it in your past.* Imagine what it was like when it happened ten days ago. It felt so good when it happened ten days ago! Completely embody that imagination. This way, you are actually accelerating the downloading of that parallel reality frequency into your present frequency output. And when your present frequency output reflects that new imagination, your reality will have to mirror that. So, actually feel what it was like ten days ago to have that revelatory moment. Wasn't it awesome? Imagine the details, like how people responded. Place it as a real-time event in your past. You can actually *change your past* by placing your desired future in your past.

This might change your desires quickly, because you will achieve them very fast. Generally, just be happy because you know that you can have anything you desire. Just place it ten days in the past or even yesterday. It doesn't matter how far in the past, as long as it's in the past. For some reason, it seems easier for people to put the achievement of their desires in their past than it is to place them right here, right now.

We are so used to focusing on our lack-based, present, physical manifestation container that, at first, all we will see is, "No, it's not here. I'm just faking it." But if we use imagination and give ourselves permission to imagine that it's in the past, then we will feel, "Oh, my desire is not here, but at least it's in the past. I can imagine that." Then it starts to feel more real, which increases your frequency. You start to feel that you own it, that you have it, that you have had it, as if it's already here. When you tap into the version of yourself that *does* have that reality, it will be reflected to you, because *that's what Creation has to do*. Creation does not have a will of its own, so it has to reflect the only will that exists, which is the free will of consciousness and its state of being. So, place everything you desire in your past, a little while ago, and feel what that was like.

So when it seems like your mind automatically places your desire in the future, then try placing it in the past. At some point, you will see everything as *present*, so when you imagine a reality that has not yet manifested in your physical container, the sense that it's not here yet starts to disappear. You feel the happiness you would feel if it was here, even though physically and logically it is not here. But you're not doing logical anymore! You are becoming more delusional— intentionally so, consciously so. Because of this, that reality will actually get a chance to manifest much quicker. So, it's a little workaround.

See It, Feel It, Be It

In general, I would suggest as a very general method that I call *"see it, feel it, be it."* Imagine what it is you desire. Imagine that version of yourself. Imagine the state of being you desire and all of the symbols that come with it. This could be as mundane as a car, or a house, or money. It could be the ability to do what you want to do whenever you want to do it. It could be a piece of land, or the partner you want to be with, or having a baby (well, be careful with that one!). Imagine anything that symbolizes your joy, your True Self, your true happiness, the true vessel of creation that you are, the true means of expressing yourself. *See it, until you start to feel it.*

The *seeing* is when your consciousness still feels like it's in this reality, but then it tunes into an alternate parallel reality, which coexists within this single timeless moment that is all of Existence. The tuning into that other reality is the seeing it, the visualizing it, the imagining it. When you imagine something and you really let go into that imagination—when you see the details of it and you give yourself permission to enjoy it as if it is real—*then you start to feel it.*

First you see it; then you feel it. The feeling of it means that you are bridging the gap between this reality and the other reality. The feeling part is the *bridge*. It's where imagination starts to download the vibratory patterns of that parallel self, that parallel version of yourself which has all of the things you desire. You start to *feel* it.

When you feel it, you begin to change; you begin to alter your vibrational field. As you alter your vibrational field, at some point it becomes so real, so vivid, that it takes over. It becomes more real to you than your present physically-manifested reality. At this point you are *being* it. You are knowing it. You are acting as if it *is*, and you are behaving and believing accordingly. So, see it, feel it, be it.

If the seeing of it is in the future, and if what still comes up for you is, "Oh, this is in the future. It is not here yet," then place it in the past. Do with it whatever you want to. Place it in the present, if you can. Then start to feel it. Do whatever you need to do to get past that seeing-feeling barrier. You need to drop into the *feeling* of it.

If you can visualize it, but you can't feel it, you are somehow blocking yourself with a belief. If this is the case, use a workaround, like placing it in your past. Be creative with it. Look into why you're resisting that image. How are you insisting that it's lacking right now? And then work around that; ease that somehow. Allow yourself to open up to where the seeing becomes the feeling. When the seeing becomes the feeling, it very quickly starts to become the being of it. And with the being of it, it's only a matter of physical time before it's very quickly reflected, physically so.

Question #3

Q: I want your help with what may be a limiting belief. There are two beliefs, actually. One is the idea that, when someone is going to punch me in the face, perhaps that punch is somehow related to my earlier thoughts, from my earlier creation.

So, the punch is still coming. And what I like about what you're saying is *although* the punch is coming, I don't have to be wed, or tethered, to the reality I'm holding about that event, to all of my past thoughts—even though there may be events *still arriving* from those thoughts.

B: Exactly. It's like an echo.

Q: Is it possible then, that some of what's arriving now is that echo?

B: Oh yes, all the time. That's why it is crucial to not take your cue from your physical circumstances, because what you are hearing and seeing is always *the past*.

Now this bridge with the past becomes thinner and thinner, and you'll start to see quicker reflections. You'll become more immediately who you actually are, even though you're in physical reality. While you are physically focused as a portion of your larger consciousness (some people call it "incarnation," but it's simply being physically focused), there will always be some difference between where you're at and what your creation shows you. There will always be a past reflection to some extent. And you will always be beyond it a little bit. But that's good; that's how you keep creating. That's why life is never stagnant.

Q: So, for example, if you were a Tibetan monk and your country was taken over, maybe that was an echo that arrived there. And it doesn't mean you're not still shifting your relationship.

B: Yes.

Q: I have a desire that we name those echoes, because otherwise when people are experiencing those echoes, they're going to get discouraged and drop your ideas.

B: Yes, exactly. And those echoes do have a name – it's "Day Two" of what I call "The Three Day Process." I'll describe it—very briefly, because you can watch it on YouTube.

The Three Day Process

The name is just a symbol: it doesn't have to be three days. It can be three minutes, three
seconds, three years. But it's a *three-stage process* that every physical creation goes through.

Day One is when you have a new vision for yourself, a new intention, a new realization: "Oh, *this* is who I am! I'm going to change my frequency. I'm going to see it, feel it, be it!"

We all have these moments. "I'm going to quit my job." "I'm going to change my relationship." It can be a significant change or even a small change, but it's something you are passionate about. You feel passion and inspiration. You're on fire. Things seem to be going very well for you on Day One; it's the "new excitement day." You're happy, you feel powerful and connected. Then, Day Two comes around the corner...

Day Two is the "day of challenge," the day of the testing of the echo, as we just discussed—the reflection of your old thoughts. Why does this happen? It's not because your Higher Self is out to get you. It actually functions like a safety switch on a gun. It's not going to allow you to pull the trigger on something that may change your entire reality until you give it the green light once more—at least once more. So, Day One is the initial signal, but you have to double that effect—sometimes triple it or quadruple it. You need to be consistent. You need to say, "This is *actually* who I wish to become. This is actually what I prefer. This is what I am ready for."

If you can't maintain your new frequency in the reflection of your old reality—your echoes—you won't be able to handle your new reality. So, it's for your own safety, for your own psyche—so that you don't go psychotic. That's why there's the safety trigger. So that's the "Day Two Challenge." An old reflection will show up: for example, your partner will doubt your decision to quit your job because of your financial situation. This will bring up your own doubts: "Yeah, yeah... maybe you're right. I should just be a realist. I remember when I believed in my dreams before, and it never worked out." Why didn't it work out? Because you always stopped at Day Two!

To get through Day Two, you have to emphasize abundance to the point where you're completely blind to lack. If you can do that, then you can maintain your frequency throughout the Day Two challenges. You will need to be completely blinded by your own frequency, to the point that you won't see, or acknowledge, a single molecule in your external "reality," You will be overpowering yourself with your own happiness. You are being delusional—yes. And if you do that with complete commitment, *your delusion will become reality.*

Actually, we're all delusional—right now! We call this "reality," but that's because we faked it for a while until it became our new reality. I call this "fake it till you make it." We think of faking it as, "Oh, that's just imagination; that's daydreaming. It's just being childish; it's delusional." Yes, but that's how you create reality; it's one of the aspects of creating your physical reality.

So throughout Day Two, the day of challenge, maintain your new frequency at all costs. Do whatever it takes. Uproot your negative beliefs and see them as positive events. If you feel something negative, it means success. It means your frequency is getting so high that this negative belief is being exposed. It no longer fits in, so you need to address it somehow. You need to look at the belief and ask, "Is this still serving me? No, I don't believe in this anymore! I believe in my happiness, that being happy will bring me everything I need. I believe my joy, my inspiration, my creativity will always be able to support me. I believe I am always supported by my Self." The old belief disappears, and you are now able to handle your new reality.

Day Three is the day of transformation, confirmation, and celebration. Your new chosen reality starts to appear.

Q: So, it can take a different amount of time, depending on your consciousness and depending on the echoes?

B: Exactly—and also depending on the perceived gravity of the new dream you are inserting. If it's to move to Cuba and become the president there, that might have a perceived gravity that doesn't equate very closely to your present reality. So, there may be more Day Two challenges in that scenario than for someone who's thinking, "Oh, I want to change my diet a little bit tomorrow." Factors like this can determine how long the time frame is. The three days are just symbolic. You could call it the "Three Stage Process" or the "Three Stages of Creation," if you prefer.

Q: **So, now my second question**.

So, there is all of Infinity expressing here (myself), and there is all of Infinity expressing out there, in the audience. How much do they have to be on board with my vision?

B: Mechanically speaking, not at all. You could shift into a parallel reality where everything is purple. They don't have to agree with that. You would simply be in a reality where they would not exist, or a different version of them would be created. You could say, "Hey, you shifted with me. Fun!" It's up to you. In a sense, you're creating your own reality all the time and it is, in that sense, individual. However, there are other consciousnesses that are embodied by the beings that we create here, in our own reflections.

So, there is some type of *actual* interaction going on every moment in which you interact with "someone," even though *your experience of it is generated out of your own energy*, and their experience, their I-AM-ness, their consciousness, projects it onto *their* screen in their particular configuration. The difference is that, for you it's completely your energy, while for them it's completely their energy. However, the interaction is still happening. There is still communication happening. There is still transformation happening. The communication is real, but the energy you experience them as, is made out of *your energy.* Otherwise, you could not experience them, because *you can only experience your own energy.*

That being said, there is also the factor that all of the consciousnesses on planet Earth (and there are many parallel planet Earths) agreed to experience a similar *collective agreement* situation, which is what we could call our "present time." We come here not only to be individuals, but also to explore what it's like to share, to communicate, and to receive. These things are all part of our individual desire, all part of our theme of exploration.

Many of us are here at this particular timing, to participate in this "time of transformation" in which we're moving from dark into light, from unconsciousness into consciousness. If it's relevant for you, if it's actually your highest desire, you will always be able to shift into whatever universe is relevant for you at any given time. You are never stuck where you are "stuck." You are only seemingly stuck here *out of choice.* As soon as that choice changes, you're good to depart. You can die, you can disappear, or whatever. You can shift into a parallel reality, a parallel collective reality. No one here has to agree with that choice, if that choice is completely relevant and genuine for you.

However (and this is my point), you came here to have a shared, collective, transformative experience. In other words, you will create the illusion of, or the experience of, collective gradual transformation in which everyone—or at least certain subgroups, certain sub-collectives—agree to move at a certain pace from darkness into light. You will be attracted to a sub-group that matches the pace at which it is relevant for you to go from darkness into light. That sub-group then becomes your entire collective.

At some point, that sub-collective becomes so totally your reality and so different from the other collectives (which are moving at different speeds) that what seems at first to be a sub-collective of the planet Earth collective, at some point will become your entire civilization, your entire collective experience. This is because you are entirely in your own parallel reality of that specific nature, and every parallel reality at this particular timing is collectively splitting off and becoming more precisely its own reality—until they are invisible to one another.

So, choose wisely—choose who you are. Become more and more of who you really are in the upcoming months and years, so you will be part of the sub-group that you actually resonate with, that actually excites you. Not that you can never change if it doesn't fully resonate—you can, you always can. But it becomes less obvious, less perceivable.

Right now, it's still very obvious that you can choose your group. You can choose your reality; you can choose to leave it, or to choose one reality out of the mixed bag that planet Earth has been in for the past few thousand years. You can do this now, at this cutting edge time when all of these sub-groups, or sub-cultures, are forming. It might not be obvious yet, but they will start to move apart from each other. This is not a bad thing; they will all go on to become their own civilizations.

So, choose your frequency for yourself as wisely as you can, and you will naturally be attracted to the sub-group that will then become your collective. In other words—you will keep up with the pace. You will gravitate together.

Q: Maybe it is the small self that has this fantasy, but I keep thinking, "Well, I'm out of here. I'm going to this other perfect realm where everyone is happy all the time."

B: Beautiful! Do you have a memory of Home?

Q: Yes.

B: That doesn't mean you didn't come here to *be here*.

Q: What I feel is that my superhero-self doesn't actually have a desire in this moment to go back to that realm. My superhero-self has a desire to hang out with these guys (the audience).

B: Exactly. That's why you're here.

Q: So, for me there's something about this collective that's super fascinating, and I feel passionate about it.

B: Yes. Beautiful. Well, there you go—it's all clear. And you can enjoy whatever you remember of your Home vibration, that non-physical state of being that you see glimpses of in physical reality and that you feel so attracted to. If someone shows a similar frequency, you fall in love with them—that kind of stuff. These glimpses are to show you who you are and where you come from—to show you what is natural, what is home, what is germane to you—so that you can merge what you see here with that. You can blend these two.

Q: Well, that's what it feels like to me. It's like the memory is not only about the past, it's also about the future. So, what I have felt or remembered is also where I'm going. And somehow I am meant to inform others about that place.

B: Simultaneously, you are also here executing more of that Home frequency. You are discovering more of that Home frequency from a place of denseness—from a place of "darkness" or ignorance—so that you can remember more and more of it to assist the collective in raising its frequency to become more like that.

Q: Exactly. And now I understand better why I wanted to ask the earlier question. I don't know if I expressed it properly. For myself, if I set up the idea that I should do a physical manifestation, doubt appears. I'm looking for proof, and if the proof doesn't occur, that can put me into a stream of doubt. What I feel instead is, "Yes, I feel that past and I feel that future," but I'm not looking for a Corvette in my parking lot tomorrow; it's not my small self's fantasies that I should see appearing. If the people in this room listen to your talk and they think, "Oh well, if I spend three days meditating on a Corvette, it will show up in my driveway," and if it doesn't show up, they're going to say, "This isn't real."

So, what I feel motivated to say is that you should somehow distinguish the types of manifestation. (Although what you're saying is absolutely true.) But what is manifesting is different than that Corvette fantasy; it's coming from a larger stream and its timing is perfect. So you have to step out of a small-self version of what it would be—otherwise you will just prove this wrong.

B: Very nice. I will elaborate on that a little bit. So, I call that "relevance"—the difference between your personal desire and what is actually relevant for you, for your theme. Sometimes I also call it "finding the balance between will and faith."

Another very important thing you touched upon is about the symbol you imagine. If that symbol is a Corvette, if that's what excites you, you must realize that it's about the *frequency* it triggers in you; the state of being that it triggers in you when you think of the Corvette. It's not about the actual car; it's not about the actual symbol. It's like the Taoist saying, "Do not mistake the finger pointing at the moon for the moon itself!" To which Bruce Lee added, "or you'll miss all that heavenly glory."

You must have a combination of the intention and the willingness to perceive what resonates for you, along with the wisdom and the faith that the *resonance* is what it's about—the frequency, the state of being, is what you really want. You want the *feeling* of it. You want the *beingness* of it. You don't want the actual representation of it. If you see it in this way, then things can manifest in a flowing way for you. You will accelerate in such a way that you get the things you actually desire—which sometimes do not end up being what you thought you wanted from a previous lower-vibratory state.

From that lower state, a Corvette may have been all you had as a symbol to represent your true heart's frequency. But once you bridge that gap and increase your frequency, once you let go of the fact that it should be a Corvette—it might be a Tesla. And that might be even better because you don't have to go to the gas station anymore. And you can go from 0 to 60 miles-per-hour in three seconds, which is pretty cool. But you also have to let go of the Tesla. Because something even better or something more relevant may show up.

Q: Yes. So, somehow surrendering to the "you" that is already existing....

B: It has already got you; it is already supporting you. Don't *insist*. Create as much as you want, but do not insist. Keep that in mind every once in a while—that you don't have to insist upon the imagery you see.

Seeing→feeling→being is a process of creation. It's an endless process of expansion. What you want is the expansion. You want to become more of the frequency of yourself. Then naturally, things will start to reflect that, exactly as they need to reflect that.

Closing remarks

Well, my friends, thank you for being here tonight. Thank you for creating and co-creating your lives in this way, to have this interaction, which is beautiful. I appreciate your Presence and your willingness. I hope you choose to be happy and in tune with yourself. I hope you start caring about your life once again.

No matter how many times you have put yourself down, no matter how many times you have blocked yourself, no matter how many times you have resisted what you deserve—to the point of feeling betrayed by Life and believing that nothing is possible—you can still get up.

It's never too late. If it was too late, you would be dead, because Consciousness does not waste resources. If you're still sitting here today, and you're breathing, and you can hear my voice—that means there's still hope for you. That means in an instant, you can switch a negative spiral around and turn it into a completely aligned, exciting, mind-blowing spiral of creation. A spiral of joy, of participation, of belonging, of being connected, of never lacking again, of being abundant, and of being Infinite. And of being in love with everything...*of being in love with yourself most of all.*

So, I hope that is your choice, or something along those lines. Make it your own, as always. Thank you.

* * * * *

Part III:

Super Accelerated Living

10 Ways to Live as a Powerful Creator

"If you devote yourself completely to any one of these ways, you will start living a super accelerated life. Things will start changing and magic will start happening. Before long, you will have so many confirmations that you will know for a fact that life is a fairytale. That's how it works, ladies and gentlemen...that's how it works. Reality is not real, it is not physical, it is not solid, it is not what-is."

- Bentinho Massaro

In this meeting, Bentinho shares ten ways in which you can make every day intensely blissful, and accelerate in the direction of your dreams. He explains how by mastering your state of being you can actually master your future.

Departing from most mainstream spirituality—with its prescribed focus on the present moment, on "what-is"—Bentinho urges us instead to flow into "future-presence." He points out that whatever appears to us in the present is inevitably a reflection of the past; it's an exact mirror image of what we've just been focusing on and, therefore, radiating out to the Universe. The Universe obliges and gives us back more of the same vibrational match!

"Do not focus on what-is," he says, "It's not spiritual. It's not enlightened. It's very, very stupid.

The present is a dead end. Future-presence is imagination—it is flow, endlessness, Infinity."

The need for passionate engagement with one's own life is the underlying theme of this final meeting, starting with the first section, *Be All-In*. If we don't care enough about our lives to move out of our comfort zones, then really none of the tools presented here will help us change our lives.

"Super-accelerated living requires that you be all-in," Bentinho says. "To *be all-in* means that your only priority is to always manage your state of being. If you wish to generate a different life, you need to start paying attention to your state of consciousness—and you *have to let go of circumstances*. You have to become aware of your vibration and learn to very, very consistently and constantly choose your preferred state of being—*regardless of what you see.*"

Exciting!

* * * * *

This meeting was streamed live on February 16, 2015 in Boulder, Colorado.

* * * * *

So...*Super Accelerated Living.* Fancy title! But if you follow these guidelines "to the T," your life will get crazy. It will get super-accelerated. So, first of all, ask yourself if this is something you want to do.

1. Be *All-In* – This is a high stakes game

I am starting with "be all-in" because none of the other tools will work for you if you don't prioritize this as a high stakes game. If you just see it as, "Meh... that's a fun thought," or if you treat it as a hobby, that won't be enough. This "game" needs to be your number-one passion. *The way you are living your life should be your number-one passion.* It's great to have other passions, but if the way you live your life—the way you manage your vibration, your state of being, your state of realization or consciousness—if this is not your number-one priority, then life will have its way with you.

When I say, "Life will have its way with you," I simply mean that your *unconsciousness* will have its way with you. If you don't show a level of commitment to the way you're living everyday life, then you are not in a vibratory state where you can handle this responsibility—the responsibility where every moment, every appearance, is owned as being a reflection of your own choices. If you can't own the fact that every experience you "run into" is a reflection of your own actions, of your state of being and your vibratory response to life, then, no offense, but you aren't ready to take on a high frequency state of consciousness. And if not, then what will take care of your life? Well, what will generate—and run—your life is everything you gathered along the way that is not yours. This is what we call *unconsciousness* or the *unconscious mind*.

If we don't step in and fulfill the role of living our lives, our unconscious mind will do it for us. That's what most people see in their everyday life: random, unintended reflections of their unconscious mind. It feels to them like "God is punishing me" or that life is a random event generator. They don't understand that *they* are generating these experiences. They have given away their power to their unconscious mind precisely because they are opting out of their responsibility. They don't want to be responsible for their state of being. It's hard work, in the sense that it requires some degree of dedication. It requires commitment, devotion, and it requires desire. *If you don't have the desire for absolute joy to enter your life on all levels of your Being, then you're not going to generate that.* You're not going to generate the necessary frequency to allow you to *consciously* take care of your life.

Everything generated in your everyday life right now is a mixture of conscious and unconscious choices. For most people, it's predominantly unconscious. If you wish to utilize that generating power and *become the power of the unconscious mind*—that which generates every single molecule in your experience, every single second of your life—then you have to step into your Creator shoes. You have to step into the vibratory state where you know that *you are responsible for the reflections you see.*

Responsible—but not in a bad way; this is not about self-judgement. It's simply about stepping up to the fact that *you desire to be master of your state of being,* master of your frequency, and master of your creation. You already are this, but you're doing so from an unconscious space that is filled with things you don't have any control over. You don't know whether you like these things or not; they're just happening from unconscious sources, from all of the random ideas you have collected over the course of your life. This is what's creating your experience, and that's why life seems so random, even meaningless, to many of you.

My life no longer seems random at all. It's very precise, very clear. And it's very obvious—or logical. Sometimes there are question marks, sometimes there are challenges, but they make sense to me. Occasionally I don't immediately see the source of some experience, where it was generated from; but it still makes sense to me—it's all part of this very streamlined, concise path. So, how have I generated this kind of purposeful life for myself? By practicing principles such as *The 10 Ways to Live as a Powerful Creator*, and by practicing them "to the T." You have to want it. You have to desire it.

So, be all-in! This is not for the faint of heart. You will run into more of your negative, limiting beliefs as you keep moving, as you keep expanding, as you keep accelerating. They will come up to the surface and be exposed. This is a good thing. As you accelerate, you will become aware of those beliefs that are holding you back, the ideas that you have hidden or avoided, or that don't make themselves known to you when you're in a mediocre state of being.

Have you ever noticed that when you're really excited and things start to accelerate, a thought comes up like, "Oh no, I can't do that! Oh my God, what would happen if I were to continue along this line?" Limiting thoughts and fears like this are *meant* to be brought to the surface. It's an *invitation* asking you: "Do you still want to hold on to this idea or are you ready to move on? Do you wish to have faith? Do you wish to have trust? Are you all-in?" *If you are all-in you can live the super accelerated life. If you are not all-in — forget about it.*

2. Be aware of your vibration and choose yours

This is perhaps the most important principle, the foundation point. Many people do not realize that they're sending out signals all of the time. Right now you're emitting a certain vibration—based on how you're defining something and how you feel about it—and I bet you aren't aware of it. Right now what are you sending out into Creation, into your reality? *You are a vibratory being;* you are a state of consciousness. So, what is your state of consciousness like? What is it emitting, radiating? What is it saying to the universe?

Please realize that what you're sending out is generating your reality—right now, actively. You cannot escape this principle, often referred to as the Law of Attraction. You can't escape the principal that 24/7 you are attracting some configuration of reality into your experience. You can't stop this mechanism. You could only stop this mechanism if you stopped existing, and I have never found anyone who could stop existing, even upon death. Existence is permanent. It is beyond time, so it has to be permanent. (What we call "permanent" from the time-bound point of view is simply "timelessness" from its own point of view.)

Since you exist, you are vibrating all the time. *All the time* you are resonating and radiating. So what are you resonating as? What are you sending out, right now? *Many people overlook this entirely, all the time; the only thing they focus on is the reflection they get back.* But the reflection you see now, is always based on your *previous* state of being, which you overlooked. And then you're stuck, because your focus is on the creation that corresponds to *your past state of being*. This is what most people see all of the time. This is what they define, what they judge, and what they base their decisions on.

Right now, you are seeing the reflections you attracted into your life by overlooking your vibration in the first place, by not paying attention. Unfortunately, it makes no sense to respond to *what you see*, or even to focus on what you see. Our society is excessively focused upon what is visible, upon what we call "reality" or what is here and now. "What-is" is king. That is the attitude, not only in mundane, everyday Newtonian understanding, but even in spiritual circles, even in mindfulness circles. "What-is" is king. Worst mistake in spirituality, ever! *Worst mistake in spirituality, ever!* What-is is a reflection of *what was*. If you focus upon what-is, you are actually focusing on the past. You are not doing your duty (not consciously anyway). You are focusing on the past, but calling it "the present."

By focusing on the past, you keep defining what you see, and you keep creating your future in accordance with your past. You generate a timeline loop that keeps repeating itself, keeps repeating itself, keeps repeating itself... ever so slightly changing your reality as you go. And that becomes the status quo of how fast a human being is "supposed" to change— very, very slowly. We are like snails with arms and legs. No offense—it's just what we've learned. It's what we teach each other on a daily basis—to overlook our current vibratory state and focus instead on the reality reflected from our *previous* vibratory state!

If you wish to generate a different life, you need to stop focusing on *what you see*, and start paying attention to your state of consciousness. If you wish to free up your consciousness, your vibration, and your feeling state—and, with that, change your circumstances very rapidly (super-accelerate your life)—*you have to let go of circumstances.* You have to become aware of your vibration and learn to very, very consistently and constantly choose your preferred state of being—*regardless of what you see.*

So that's the starting point: be aware of what you are sending out in the first place. What are you sending out right now? How do you feel? What are you thinking? What are you defining? What are you believing? Be aware of this! Don't overlook what you are generating right now, because what you are feeling now is what you are going to attract to yourself. This is just the way it is. You can call it "New Age," but it's just the way it is.

3. Keep planting new seeds *constantly* – Be in the state of imagination

Learn to be in the non-physical and constantly "plant new seeds"—with the emphasis on "constantly." How do you do this? By living more in your imagination than living in what-is. "Oh my God! How terrible! How could you say such a thing? We are not supposed to deny what-is." The worst sin in many people's minds is to deny what-is and to be in imagination. People think, "That's the stupidest, most irresponsible thing you can do!" No. It's not—it's the most exciting thing you can do. It's how kids live.

Just observe young children at play, and you'll see that they live mostly in the non-physical. What they're focusing on is their state of being—creating non-stop from their imagination, from what they see in "the mind's eye." You don't see children focused on the circumstances and the logistics and the have-to's and how-to's. They're still in the original state of consciousness, which is non-physically focused, and which understands that the physical focus, or the physical reflection, is simply a natural expression of the non-physical state that came before it.

If you are always in the imaginative state, then you are always in the super-accelerated way of living. You will attract to yourself the things you desire much more rapidly than everyone around you—way faster than those who are focused on what-is, and who therefore keep recreating the past into the future, calling it "the present." *The present is always the past.* Do not focus on what-is. It's not spiritual. It's not enlightened. It's very, very stupid.

Focus, instead, on what you want to see; see only your preference. Learn to do just this one trick. In fact, if you practice even one of these principles "to the T," all the way... if you devote yourself completely to any one of these points (well, let's say two of them, just to have some variety), you *will* start living a super accelerated life. Things will start changing and magic will start happening. Before long, you will have so many confirmations that you will know for a fact that life is a fairytale. That's how it works, ladies and gentlemen—that's how it works. Reality is not real, it is not physical, it is not solid, it is not what-is.

So, keep planting new seeds constantly. How do you do that? Right now, ask yourself what excites you the most to imagine? Many people have blocked themselves from accessing their excitement: "What do you mean, what excites me the most? Yeah, I can imagine something but...?" Don't quibble—just start practicing it. At some point, you'll get glimpses that hit the right spot. You'll imagine something and suddenly feel, "Ahhhh!" And a wave of bliss will come over you. That's the state we are supposed to be in *all of the time*. That's why we are here. That's how we are designed. We are "Children of God," so be in God.

If at any time you're focused on what-is, and you notice your vibration is sort of mediocre or low or even "just fine, good, nice," know that this is all *very low*. You don't want that! You don't want nice, you don't even want great. You want *amazing*! You want crazy, over-the-top, blissed-out excitement. You want to be on fire. You want to be *alive*—that's why you were born! That's why you chose to be here: to create, to expand, to play, to have fun, to enjoy. You came here to overwhelm your experience with your chosen creation, your chosen theme, your chosen blueprint, your chosen intention, your chosen quality of consciousness.

What is your desired quality of consciousness? Imagine everything that comes with that, everything that symbolizes it. It can be something as simple as a new car, but it can also be something as subtle and seemingly spiritually-inclined as a non-dual state of being or self-realization, like Buddha. It doesn't matter; it can be anything. In my eyes, these two things—a car or a non-dual state—are equally as "enlightened." At some point, you will lose complete sense of what "enlightenment" is. If you are truly living as yourself, you have no clue as to what it is. It disappears from view! If there's still such a thing as enlightenment, you are not enlightened. So, to be enlightened, drop all judgement, drop all bias, and simply know that *all of life, all of Creation, is equally valid.*

Now, with the understanding that all of Creation is equally valid, what is it that you would draw the most excitement from right now? If you could imagine it. Can you find something? Tune into your vibration. Be aware of your state of being right now and see what you're sending out. What are you vibrating as right now? And then what would you like that to become? How would you like to feel instead? Remember, the way you feel right now is going to attract a physical reality that represents that exact state of being. So, if you don't feel good right now, you are ensuring that your future will look ugly.

Who do you want to be in control—your unconscious mind or your conscious choice? It's up to you. And it's all equally valid. You can create a random reality for the rest of your life and not know who you are, not feel worthy of desiring what you desire, and not feel worthy of creating what you want. But please, know that *you came here to be worthy of creating what you desire.* That is your sole purpose. You can pretend to be selfless by not desiring what you desire, but you are actually being very, very arrogant by doing so. Embrace desire, embrace what you love, embrace your passions, embrace what you really want. When you embrace desire, you are in tune with your Higher Self, so you're actually being *non-arrogant.* You're being transparent, and you're actually being free.

4. Don't WAIT – Don't monitor the germination process

So, always keep planting new seeds. But don't stick around to watch them grow—don't monitor the germination process. In other words, never wait. If you are constantly generating new seeds of consciousness, new ideas, new imagined scenarios—if you stay constantly in the imagination state—then you are automatically not waiting to see what happens to the seeds you planted before this moment.

What often happens is that you imagine something new and it excites you, and then physical manifestations start showing up, giving you evidence of your imaginative power. Someone might call you up with information about the very thing you were just thinking about an hour before like, "Oh hey, I've got this job for you…" "Oh awesome! That's exactly what I wanted." Then, what happens for most people is that they get stuck on that one single thing. "Oh yes, I manifested something—Boom!" So, they start to watch how it grows, which is the best way to kill your seed. This is *waiting*. When things start showing up, don't wait for them to fully blossom—create something else. Generate something new. I call that being in "Future-Presence" which I'll discuss in point #6.

Constantly, constantly, constantly plant new seeds. Don't stop! At first it might seem hard because you can only think of one or two things that you desire. But I promise that as you kick-start this, you will reactivate more and more of your passion. And the more you are connected, the more you are able to carry newer, higher vibrations, the more you are able to carry the torch of The One's desire to express itself in all possible ways. Your body, your mind, your circumstances, your life, your finances, your re-sources, your relationships—will all take on a tone of being able to carry a greater flow of frequency, a greater amount of abundance. More and more dreams will be made manifest through this facet of Consciousness, this "being" that we call "you," be-cause you are opening up to your authentic desires.

The more you do this, the more desires you will generate. Don't be afraid of this! At some point, you will learn to be in a state of desire all of the time, without filtering it through the idea that there can be lack. Then, the state of desire itself will fuel you. So, re-own what you already are, which is the Creator, and master your state of being. Become precise, become exact, become clear. Become desirous of being desirous, desirous of being in a state of clarity, desirous of knowing who you are.

Right now, you may associate the state of desire with pain, with: "I don't have what I want" or "There is a gap between where I am now and where I want to be." But the more you embrace the idea of desire, the more you get lost in the energy of desire—in the energy of imagination—the more you will start to access greater abundance and depth of desire. More expansive visions will come to you—things you couldn't think of before, things you never knew you would want. Suddenly, you will start to desire these things! This is a beautiful phenomenon; it's not ugly in any way. When you reach this point, having desires won't cause you suffering anymore because you will have transcended the idea that there could be lack. You will be in the abundant state of desire itself, having mastered your state of being in the Now.

5. Care more about how you feel than what you manifest

Another way people tend to drive themselves into the ground a little bit is by thinking they desire *the thing* they desire more than they desire *the desire itself*. People think they want the object—the car, or the realization, or the community, or the relationship, or the finances—more than they want the *feeling state* that is represented or symbolized by these images, notions, concepts, and manifestations.

Over time you will learn, through burning your hands every once in a while, that *what you truly want is to feel good*. This is a sign of maturity. From here, things start shifting for you very quickly because you are no longer attached, you are no longer childish or needy, and you are no longer projecting as much (if at all). You simply become very clear and decisive and grounded in your own self-fulfillment. You know that you are your own God. You are now the chooser, and you can master your state of being at any given moment. It is up to you—you have free will, you have choice.

So start to realize that what you are after is the *feeling state*, rather than the circumstance or the manifestation. Manifestation is great; it's awesome! But it primarily serves as evidence for the fact that *you* are awesome. Every manifestation is simply confirming your epic ability to create your reality. It's not about tying yourself down or attaching yourself to that thing you generated. The thing is only there as proof, as a little nudge and encouragement to remind you, to prove to you: "Yes! *I am the creator of my reality.* Now what do I want to generate next? And what do I want to generate next?"

"But to what end?" some people might ask. "Doesn't it end up as an endless cycle of desire and frustration and greed?" No! There is nothing more beautiful than to be in a state of pure desire, knowing that you are connected to All-That-Is, knowing that you are infinitely powerful and infinitely abundant. That state itself becomes your home. That state itself becomes your freedom, your liberation, your source of power and well-being. It becomes your ability to manifest the things you desire quickly, quickly, quickly. That state itself *is* super-accelerated living.

What must become most important to you is not what you get in your life, but *how* you are living your life, how you are feeling across all of it. As soon as you can prioritize this, as soon as you gain that wisdom, everything will start to change and accelerate. Because now your source of stability is no longer your tension, or your money, or your safety switch, or your government, or any of these systems you have relied on, based on your unconsciousness. Your source of stability is now *you*. Your state of being is now under your control in the most positive way possible. *You are now in complete control.*

6. Constantly be in the Future-Presence state

Again, I am using the word "constantly." I want to inspire you to *constantly* desire to stay alert and be aware of what you are sending out, until you reach a super-satisfactory state where your life is no longer generated randomly, but consciously.

Constantly be in the future-presence state (or the non-physical focus). What is future-presence? As I explained, the present is actually the past. So then, what is the present? It is the future. How does that work? When you're in the future with your consciousness—in other words, when you're generating a state of being that you enjoy, utilizing images that don't seem to be "here"—you become very present to the nature of consciousness. You become very present to the fact that you *exist* right here, right now. You become very present to being alive. Your vibratory state becomes very conscious, which is Presence. To be in the future, generates more Presence than to be in the present—which is based on the past.

If you don't fully believe this, ask yourself, "When do I feel more alive and joyful? When I'm imagining something that excites me, or when I'm focused on some task in the here and now?" Which creates a better feeling state? What makes you feel more present to yourself, more present to the fact that you exist, to the fact that you're alive and that you are a vehicle through which the Creator expresses itself? When do you feel more aligned, more connected— when you're in the imaginative state, which other people call "the future" or "unreal," or when you're in the "real" state, which your parents adore, because they feel somewhat safe that you're taking care of your life? Which state feels more enjoyable, more alive?

The degree of joy you feel is exactly proportionate to the degree of Presence you have in that moment. The more joyful you are, the more naturally present you are to the fact that you exist, to the fact that you are inseparable from Existence.

So, be in the state of future-presence, in order to not be in the present! The present is a dead end. It kills you. It's death. Future presence is imagination. It is flow, endlessness, Infinity. That is Presence.

When I say "Be in the state of future-presence," it's the same as saying "Be in the state of imagination." It's also another way of saying "Keep planting new seeds constantly." So you see the important role imagination plays in super-accelerated living. Imagination is 99.9999% of your being. To dismiss 99.9999% of your being is a recipe for unhappiness.

To re-embrace that portion of your consciousness as an equally valid portion of who you truly are, and to utilize this very powerful tool, is a recipe for happiness, joy, expression, and creation.

So #5 "Constantly be in the future-presence state" means be in imagination or the non-physical focus. It means don't get stuck in the physical focus because it has nothing to tell you except that you created your present reality. If you don't like what you see, it's also telling you that you overlooked the vibration you were previously sending out. If you *do* like what you see, it's a little nudge, like, "Hey, great job yesterday being in that good feeling state. Amazing! Keep doing it." And you respond with a simple thanks; don't respond with "Wow, let me hold on to this amazing manifestation." No—keep moving on! Take it and leave it. Take it and leave it.

This is why it's a high stakes game: it requires that you keep on moving. It requires that you keep on imagining, that you're always ready to be in the non-physical state of creating the next moment that you desire and that feels good.

7. Trust your Higher Self

Trust your Higher Self, or whatever you prefer to call it. You can call it life, you can call it God, you can call it Higher Mind, or non-physical mind, or non-physical Consciousness, or the Universe—it doesn't matter. But trust the Greater Self, your Higher Self. This means to *let go of how and when things should manifest*. If you notice there is tension regarding how things should manifest or when things should manifest (as proof that you are creating your reality), then you are not maturing. You are not allowing yourself to mature in terms of principle #5 "Care more about how you feel than What You Manifest."

If you notice tension or attachment toward a future outcome, remember that what you truly want is to feel good. *What you truly want is to feel good!* When it comes to seemingly big manifestations that we have always associated with happiness and freedom, I know it's very hard to choose the feeling state over the manifestation. Let's say you are offered 20 million dollars. For many people, this is a trigger to become attached to the manifestation. But really, all this is saying is, "Good job. Now move on. Good job. Continue—expand even more." But if you are offered 20 million dollars with the choice that you can either take the money or you can feel good, you would probably take the 20 million dollars, right? Which is fine. I would do the same thing because I already know how to feel good. So, I'll take the 20 million.

But my point is, if you had to choose one over the other, which one would you take? You can either have 20 million dollars for the rest of your life—it doesn't matter how much you spend; you will have always 20 million dollars in your bank account—or you can always feel good. Which one would it be? Why do you want the 20 million dollars? The answer is: To feel good!

So it's obvious—we all know that happiness is not found in the manifestation. Everyone is taught this through cheesy bumper stickers but there are very few of us who have actually gained the clarity and maturity to prioritize state of being. And here is the thing: if you really prioritize how you feel, your focus starts to shift naturally and automatically from the physical to the non-physical, from the what-is to future-presence. Effortlessly, you start to generate all of the things you've always desired but that you resisted by having such a tense grasp on the physical. So, learn the maturity, learn the wisdom of really appreciating and being grateful for the moments when you feel really, really good, and let that fill you up. Let that be your freedom, *let that be the confirmation* that you are being successful vibrationally, energetically, spiritually, and consciously. Feeling good is *always* the highest.

8. Focus on what works and what has worked

It's hard sometimes not to notice physical reality. It's okay to notice it, but that should be all you do. Notice it, but don't linger. Many people linger on their physical manifestation and get too deeply focused on what isn't working. When we focus too much on what isn't working, we tighten up our vibration, we densify our vibration, we become solid again. We become linear and limited, and we feel separate. We feel like we are lacking, and that we actually are not an infinite creature. So instead, focus on what works and what has worked.

As soon as you shift your attention to what is working and what has worked for you in the past, you start to notice an immediate shift in your vibration, in your frequency state, in your feeling state. You feel more expanded; you feel like you have intuitive access to everything you need to have access to at any moment. You are again prioritizing your feelings over everything else. This will then speed up your acceleration in this manifestation game of creation.

9. Ask what's most important to you every day upon waking up

When we wake up in the morning, there's a moment before all the random shit comes rushing back in. In this moment, we have a powerful opportunity. This moment offers us a clean, clear slate where we can insert our intention for that day. It sounds a little cheesy, but it works.

In exactly that waking moment each day, ask what is most important to you. Don't wait. Don't wait! Don't go take a pee first. Lie there, even if your bladder is about to explode, and ask yourself, "What is most important to me right now?" At some point, you can do this while you're peeing, but for the sake of practice, simply lie in your bed, suffer a little bit, and ask yourself what is most important to you. Do this every day. Like right now, *this* day. Really tune into it. "How do I wish to experience this day?"

If you do this, you will see *major* differences. The difference between a bad day and a good day indeed is like that expression, "I got up on the wrong side of the bed." Exactly—this is a very apt description. If you get up on the wrong side of the bed, the negative spiral, the negative ideas, the physical-present focus is what rushes back in. If that becomes your intention, then you're going to have a bad day. However, if you keep that at bay, if you avoid that altogether, ignore it, and—because you *are* God—you *insert* the vibratory state of your choice, the intention of your choice, then *your entire day will flow.* Try it out!

10. Always feel good and confident

This is all you need to know, really. This is the summary: *Always feel good and confident.*

If you can do only this! Always do this. And I do mean always, I do mean constantly, I do mean consciously, I do mean deliberately. *I do mean that you have to care about how you feel; you have to care about your life.* Always feel good and confident. If you can manage just this! I know it's not always easy, but it's very simple and it *is* by choice. Try it. You will become better at it very rapidly, depending on the level of your desire to actually feel good, rather than to have things you want.

Maturity is required to understand the importance of always choosing to feel good—no matter what! You need a level of maturity where you prioritize feeling good over any other consideration—no matter what your thoughts suggest to you, no matter what physical-present reality suggests to you. You just want to feel good, and each morning you wake up setting this intention. You place yourself in the non-physical, imaginative seed of consciousness. You are always creating the next moment, never lingering in the present. You are never monitoring how your past seeds are germinating. "Well, let me wait here. What did I create? Will it come about?" That is *waiting*; it's a waste of energy. It makes you spiral downward instead of continuing to expand.

Again, super accelerated living requires that you be all-in. *To "be all-in" means that your only priority is to always manage your state of being.* It may sound negative, but it's actually very positive. Once you get the hang of this, there's no going back. You have clearly seen that you generate your state of being all the time and that your circumstances are an immediate reflection of that. And hooray! You live in a collective timeline where we are giving ourselves, as a collective species, increased permission to become more slippery, to become faster, to have less of a gap between state of being and manifestation.

Some of my days recently have been insane—literally insane. And I wish the same for you—because there's no going back. Once you taste this, you forget all about spirituality. You forget all about non-duality and self-realization. All you will know is that you are God—that you are creating, and you are in bliss, and you are one with All-That-Is. You will realize that you have access to infinite abundance, that you are living your passion, and that you are infinitely worthy of being you—in whatever way you desire to be you.

*   *   *   *   *

A Note on integrity

I've spoken in the previous two meetings (Part I and II) about how integrity is maintained when applying manifestation techniques. Here are a few more thoughts on this topic.

Integrity comes naturally and effortlessly, but in a very free, even rebellious, sort of way at times—depending on how stuck other people insist on being. But you will have a high degree of clarity and integrity and love for other people, *naturally*, because you are overflowing. You aren't fooled by any of their stories of lack; integrity doesn't mean you agree with others' statements of lack: "Oh, you can't do that, that's way too awesome." You remain free; you are ungraspable.

In fact, you're very annoying to many people because they can't grasp you, they can't anchor you to the floor, or bring you down to their level of lack. To have integrity and compassion doesn't mean you go down another person's rabbit hole. It means you stay true to the example you are, by being in the vibratory state you desire. It doesn't mean you kill or rape people or get whatever you want from other people. It doesn't mean you deprive others of what they desire in order to indulge in your own gratifications—those kind of "lower state wants" that are just excuses for not being in bliss already, by choice.

This is not about getting your gratifications from someone else or depriving someone else. It's simply about maintaining your own frequency to such a degree that you are overflowing. You are confident to an annoying degree—very lovingly so, very skillfully so—but also sometimes annoyingly so. But that's okay. It's good; it's what you want. You are naturally, automatically annoying—you're not *trying* to be annoying. You are simply being yourself. But that annoys a lot of people because they're not allowing *themselves* to be themselves, so why should you? The more annoying you are, in a sense, the more free you are, the more you are actually in alignment with who you truly are. You are actually providing contrast for people; showing them that they need to match that vibration within themselves.

So, you are a healer. The more annoying you are, the better healer you are. If you're a very, very pleasant healer, you're not a very good healer. I'm talking about "everyday healing," not giving a session: "Okay, I put my hands on you, you go back home and you feel a little better." I'm talking about the true example of healing. True healing is being completely in alignment with yourself—to the point where you can always choose to be in bliss, regardless of circumstances. This is what you emit, what you radiate. As you radiate, that high-frequency vibration will bump into lower frequency vibrations for whom it's relevant to step into your field and be annoyed. That's a good thing; people's annoyance is an indication that your vibration is getting to them, and showing them what's possible. The result is annoyance for a little while, until they realize they can do it, too. Then *they* become annoying. But not to you! They become your friend because they're now a vibratory match.

So, that's how it works. *Be yourself. Always feel good and confident.*

* * * * *

Q&A

Question #1

Questioner: Can you describe some of the craziness you experienced on a daily basis recently?

Bentinho: Well, a lot of it is non-physical and beyond my ability to really explain or share in words that make sense. A lot of it is vibratory stuff, like expansions and bliss and all that. But on a physical level, I can say that within a time span of six days, I have gone from one reality—meaning living in a million dollar house, paying a certain amount of rent—to suddenly having the idea to move back in with some of my crew mates. This very spontaneous, random thought came up for us and we said, "Let's get a mansion." And two days later, we've seen a place and now we're actually going to save $12,000 a year by moving into a $4.5 million dollar house.

That is just one example, but everything—little details, like furniture, and communication, and offers from banks—everything conspires in a single day to make things happen. Then, the very next day, you look back upon your life and everything has changed. The day before, you had no clue. This happens more and more on a daily basis: you're in a constant state of bliss, and you're getting constant confirmations, constant proof that the sky is the limit.

Lack of means is not an issue

Many people get stuck, and this is something I'd like to discuss. When it comes to super accelerated living, a lot of people deal with the issue of lack of means— lack of means to do what they wish to do or to create what they wish to create. We feel stuck due to the circumstances we focus upon. This is all based on the fact that you believe there is only one physical reality and that there are only X amount of things inside of that reality. You forget that there are *infinite parallel realities*, and whatever reality you desire already exists. You can't steal it from anyone, you can't give it to anyone; you can only experience the reality that you are generating, the reality that you are a vibrational match to.

There is infinite abundance. Many people feel guilty when it comes to money, when it comes to creating what they desire, because automatically (based on their erroneous view of reality) they think, "The more I get, the less someone else gets." Nothing is further from the truth. The more you get, the more everyone else gets, because you are able to give and to share. People are "arrogantly ironic" (let's call it that) when they wish to save the world, when they wish to be selfless, because the way they think they can be selfless and of service is by depriving themselves of the things they desire. This is the worst thing you can do for mankind.

It reinforces the idea that lack exists and that we have to keep generating lack as a collective. It reinforces to other people that they should also deprive themselves, and that as soon as they stand out of the crowd, we will judge them: "Oh, how dare you be so happy?" But wait a second... didn't you *want* them to be happy? Is that why *you* are not happy—because you wanted to *help them* to be happy? Now they're happy and you're not happy about them being happy because they should be serving other people by being unhappy!

This is a very erroneous mind loop that many people are caught in unconsciously. They don't understand the irony; they don't see how erroneous these ideas are.

You have to rise above the crowd and dare to create the reality you desire. In fact, that's the only thing you *can* do; that's why you're here. You have already generated your current reality, whatever that may be, as abundantly as I have generated mine. You may be living in a tent, which is not less than a $4.5 million dollar house; I'm not saying that. But if you're living in a tent and you *don't like* living in a tent, but you do so because you believe that you *should* live in a tent—

because it's the eco-friendliest way to live or it's the most selfless way to be an example to other people—then you are caught in a loop. But, if this is all exciting to you, then it's absolutely perfect: you are doing exactly what I'm doing in a different way.

What's exciting to me is to show the world that there's no limit—that at 26 you can live in a $4.5 million dollar house. I'm not doing this to prove anything, but this is my natural theme, this is my natural flow—to live large, to live adventurously. And to not be afraid to find the loopholes in the system—loopholes meaning creative, non-traditional ways to access amazing things, without being wealthy. But people are stuck in believing they have to wait for the means.

Keep planting new seeds constantly, and don't watch them germinate. That's what I do. So, whether I got this house or not, doesn't matter. Where I'm at, what I'm creating is the very next thing that excites me. Naturally, the trail I leave behind is the trail of manifestation. The Law of Attraction will put that trail behind me; I don't have to worry about the how's and the when's of that trail, because what I prioritize is feeling good. Because that feels so much better even than when I get what I *think* I want. The more you notice this, the more you will learn to operate this way. It's simply a matter of wisdom—gaining wisdom through contrast, through bumping into your experience over and over again until you know: "I want to feel good, and when I feel good, I get everything I desire in physical reality so quickly, so effortlessly, and in even better ways than I imagined possible."

Super accelerated living means that you're always in Future-Presence, you're always free, you're always generating what you desire. You're never feeling guilty, and if you do, you recognize it's a limiting belief and move on. There's no guilt, because you understand that by generating exactly what you want, you are able to give that much more of who you truly are.

Many people are waiting for resources in order to make their preferred life happen. They are very focused on what they *have*. If you're focused on what you have, your state of being will reflect what you have, which is limited. What will you attract in the future? More of what you have. So, if you wish to have less limitation, you have to be more imaginative. You have to raise your frequency to a feeling state of absolute certainty that anything can happen and that you are meant to generate happiness for yourself— and for others as a natural by-product.

Don't go by the system of social norms, rules, and regulations. Don't get caught in ideas of logic and reasoning and linear reality that block you from being open to things coming your way in unpredictable, surprising, non-linear, non-physical, non-governmental ways. We are all so focused on the government. "Oh, the government does this, the government will do that, the government will take care of me. I'll save my money until I'm old enough and then I'll get it back." Don't depend on the system. Generate your own system! You are meant to be your own government, your own God. You are meant to be your own support system.

The government would not exist if we weren't so lame, OK? We're all lame—very lame, very lazy vibrational beings! We don't take responsibility for creating our own life. People say, "The government has so much power over us." Well, that power is a direct physical reflection of us saying, "No, thank you. I don't want to take care of myself. I don't want to live my own life, I don't believe I can do the things I want to do. I'm not worthy, so you do it for me. Then I can see you on television, pretend it's real, and blame you for everything that goes wrong in my life."

However, it's possible for you to switch that around. You can realize that you're meant to be your own governmental system. Your life can be in your own hands. You can live on an island. Literally and metaphorically, energetically you can live on an island where no cop will ever enter, where no government will ever interfere, where no outside authority will ever know about you because they don't have to. You can live free, creating your own reality and supporting yourself. How? By relying on your vibrational attitude, relying on your own mastery. As soon as you learn to take care of your own vibration, the manifestation will show you that you're free of outside authority.

Be fearless and remain unattached

There are so many creative ways to manifest what you desire without having to wait for the traditional means to get it. But you have to be willing to be fearless; *you have to be willing to take risks, to be all-in!* It's a high stakes game. You have to be willing to go all-in every single day, and if you do, you will be rewarded. This will happen because you're not holding back energetically, because you're not relying on an external system—on your unconsciousness in other words. Instead, *you're relying on your consciousness.* You're saying, "I can handle this. I can consciously choose to feel good."

Of course, be watchful of your process, and honor wherever you are at. Don't overstep your limits, but do try to move beyond your comfortable boundaries and see how far you can get away with it. If you start to collapse or really doubt yourself, then take a step back, re-assimilate, observe, take some time, take a shower. Stop creating as intensely for a while; don't live as super-accelerated for a few days. Take a step back and relax. Observe all that happened and all that came up for you, including your subtle belief systems. Start un-mixing your frequencies, making them more precise, more conscious, more God-like, more powerful, more joyful, more self-sufficient, and more self-fulfilling.

Then step it up a bit once again, applying the guidelines I presented here, the "Ten Ways to Live as a Powerful Creator." If you do, your life will become an insane reflection. People will be baffled when they see you a year later. They'll be like, "What did you do? What's going on here? Did you rob a bank?" I had a friend that came to my current house and he said, "What kind of scheme do you have going on here?" Actually, your life can be a good example; people see what's possible and start thinking, "If you can do it, I can do it."

Am I saying that you need to create your life in some kind of epic way? No, you don't need to at all. It's just a natural by-product, to a certain degree, depending on how relevant it is for your theme. For my theme right now, it feels very relevant to expand in that particular way, as a by-product. But I'm not fooled by it, not sidetracked by it. I'm not materialistically focused, because as soon as one gets materialistically focused, one loses touch with one's non-physical nature, *which is where the abundance comes from.*

So literally, what I'm looking at when I see mani-festations happen so quickly for me, and in such seemingly non-logical, non-linear ways, is the effortless manifestation of where I am holding my vibration, my center of alignment. But I'm staying here, even as I witness it. This doesn't mean I don't get excited, or don't ever yell, "Yeaaaaaaaah!" But even when I do, *I feel that I am my environment, and there is no separation.* I'm not going to think, "Oh, I'm dependent on this physical matter, this piece of brick. This amazing set of bricks with this amazing view somehow determines my happiness, my vibratory state." Because then, as soon as it burns to the ground or I lose it for some reason, I lose my vibration along with it.

As soon as you get too attached to the physical manifestation, your Higher Self is smart enough to take it away from you, because it's teaching you how to be a vibrational master, not how to hold on to brick and cement. It's teaching you how to be free. Once you understand how to be free, once you understand that what you truly want is to feel good, then the manifestation will happen right in front of your eyes. You will look at it and engage with it, and feel happy about it. You will feel at one with it and feel love through it. At the same time you'll feel absolutely free from it. It is never yours, even though you own it, and even though you feel like you own it vibrationally. It is actually your creation, and in that sense you own it, but you don't hold on to it because what you truly own is infinite abundance, infinite means, and infinite possibilities. That is a way more exciting manifestation than just one aspect of it in physical form.

So, this is the way you can live both attached and non-attached. Free. Not attached to non-attachment, but naturally unattached because what you are really attached to is your vibratory state, your alignment.

Question #2:

I'm curious about where you came from and where you began to develop this within yourself. Can you sketch out a trajectory of your life so far?

B: Well, I can try, but actually it's difficult for me to sketch out a brief trajectory because it's very multi-dimensional, very timeless, and very parallel. It becomes harder and harder for me to see from a linear point of view. I am God, and so are you. Anything is possible. I could tell a physical story of how I grew up, but that seems so uninteresting and so unreal, so "not me" anymore.

So briefly then, I grew up in Amsterdam, in Holland, with two awesome parents. I'm 26 years old right now. At the age of 16, I had a really strong desire to find out who I am, what is the source of life, and what is possible. So, I read a ton of books. I went to India for half a year and sat with teachers and swamis. I meditated and rebelled and absorbed and extracted and transcended and then left all that behind me. Very rapidly, I started to gain real clarity as to how reality works, as to who I am, what is true, what's not true, what is permanent, and what's not permanent. I went through a process of what you could call "enlightenment" or "self-realization."

I always had the teacher in me so I naturally shared whatever I knew, and that just simply developed. I started doing some YouTube videos and was invited to the United States to share this message with people. Back in the day, it was more traditional non-duality; it was more about recognizing the changelessness of Presence or Awareness that we are. My teaching has changed many times over the past say, five years; I've seen at least six significant changes,

I always had this idea of creating an online academy where everything can be sequential, step-by-step, and where all I've learned can be brought down to very simple step-by-step terms for the masses. Last year I felt ready to do that; I felt that my teachings had reached a level of readiness or completion, in a sense. There was a wholeness to them, where I knew I could write them down, without two years later feeling like, "Awww, this is terrible." I'm sure I will make some changes along the way, but the whole picture is complete enough to where I can say right now—even though my teachings keep refining and evolving— that it's a very holistic system for everyone. The average Joe can go through step-by-step.

I started creating the Trinfinity Academy about half a year ago, in late 2014. And now…well, I'm here. There is so much I didn't tell you but that's okay; I don't know what else to say. If you have any specific questions, I'm always open to answering anything about my personal life. So, feel free to ask as specifically as you want, whether it is about relationships, money, or whatever. It doesn't matter.

Question #3:

I've been following your videos and gaining a lot; it was wonderful. But two days ago something took me out. I don't know what it is, but I have come back to a very familiar anxiety.

It feels like a tension inside. I do things to get away from it—I drink, take painkillers. It doesn't feel good to do that anymore, but it also doesn't feel good to feel this feeling. I watched another video this morning, and I came to an awareness that **I have a belief that I am unworthy**, which is something you speak about a lot. I kind of broke down and wept. So, here I am now.... I still have the tension and I don't know how to embrace it fully and have it disappear. I don't know if my desire for whatever I want is very strong in this moment, but I do want to feel good and find my peace.

Bentinho: What are you believing that your spirit disagrees with? Because that's why you feel bad.

Q: That I can't possibly understand this. Or if this is it, it's too simple – so this can't be it.

B: Does that feel good?

Q: No.

B: Then it must not be true.

Q: Right.

B: But even though you know it's not true, do you still think it will serve you in some way to hold onto believing something that's not true? How will it serve you to continue to believe that you can't understand this? Or that you can't do this? Or that you can't make this yours?

Q: I suppose it won't serve. It's not serving me in a pleasant way.

B: Good. But you hold onto it because you *believe* it serves you. There's no other reason to hold onto anything. You're holding on because you think it will give you benefit or safety or security, or that it will help you to avoid something even more negative. We often make ourselves feel bad in order to avoid feeling worse. The best way to feel worse, though, is to feel bad! Because then you generate more bad feelings and more bad feelings. So, if you really wish to avoid feeling bad, you have to *choose* to feel good— no matter what the circumstances look like, no matter what your mental capacity looks like.

Q: Feeling unworthy is arrogant—would you say that?

B: I would. Innocent but arrogant. It's a form of arrogance. To feel unworthy is to basically state that you are not created by the Creator. To feel unworthy is to say that somehow you, and you alone—out of trillions upon trillions upon trillions of beings, trillions of I-AM individuations of the All-That-Is-Consciousness—somehow only you managed to enter this Creation from outside of Creation. Isn't that arrogant?

In other words, everything is worthy of being a part of Creation, but somehow, when you were born—I don't know how it happened—but you came from outside of Creation. You just dropped into Creation from outside of Creation. In other words, you are not a portion of Existence. In other words, Existence does not desire you. "Existence doesn't desire me" is the feeling of unworthiness. It's the translation of: "I believe that Existence does not desire me to be who I am." Why would the One Existence create a portion of itself that it doesn't want to be here? That could only happen if there were two beings. If there were two beings, one could do something that the other disagrees with. Since there is only one Existence, Existence cannot do anything that it disagrees with. So, you are saying Existence disagrees with you, which implies that you must come from somewhere other than Existence. That is arrogant.

Q: After your last talk, I had the experience that I was connected—that I am you and I love you and I want to serve all of you. That feeling left. Something happened that seemed to undo this connection and I haven't been able to recollect exactly what it was.

B: The connection is not undone; you simply started to send out a different message, a conflicting vibratory state. Can you pinpoint what that is? That would be helpful. Can you sense what are you sending out right now? Because you're only covering over the connection that is always there; it can't actually be disconnected. Again, that would mean you're not part of Existence; that would mean you could connect or not connect. But then, who are you if not Existence? You can't escape Existence. You're always going to be God and inseparable from God. So, you are always desired, you can't make a mistake. You can only be yourself, you can only add to the expansion of the Universe. Anything you do, no matter how much you fuck up, it is all expanding the Universe; it is all Infinity expressing itself in all the ways that it can.

From the Infinite One's point of view, what we call "fucking up" is nothing but adding more layers to

Creation, the addition of more ways in which The One can express itself to itself. That is all it sees. It's a positive thing to mess up. There are no mistakes; you can *only* add to Creation, you can only serve, you can only co-create, you can only add to clarity, to Consciousness, you can only add to Creation. There is no way you could ever do anything wrong. Doing something wrong is a perfectly positive manifestation of Existence. It is adding to The One knowing itself.

So you're always being of service simply by being you. Whether you judge that as positive or negative is up to you, but through the eyes of The One it's always positive. You are always adding. Every second you are adding a thought, every second you are adding a feeling, every second you are adding a new context, a new relationship, a new way in which it can know itself; a way in which it hasn't known itself before. So, you're always positive, always desired, and always appreciated. Your presence is always adding to the expansion of the Universe. Does it make you feel more connected when you think along those lines?

Q: In part it does. And I have the idea that there are still beliefs that I'm holding onto, like I'm powerless and ineffective.

B: Beautiful. Does that make you feel a certain way?

Q: Yes.

B: Isn't that a sign of power? You generated a feeling by using a thought. Isn't that power?

Q: Yes.

B: Nice. So, what if you have a different type of thought—would you create a different type of feeling? And with that, a different type of action and a different type of reality?

Q: Yes.

B: So, are you not powerful? Are you not already creating how you feel right now? And with that, everything else, because the feeling is the vibratory state. How could you do that if you were not a part of God, and if you did not possess a portion of its power to create?

Q: I am creating how I'm feeling in this moment, but I still have parts of my life that aren't the way I want them.

B: Well, how many things have you thought in the past that were out of alignment?

Q: Many.

B: Well, there you go. See how powerful you are? All of these parts of your life that you don't enjoy are proof of how powerful you are—just not in the way that you want to be. But nevertheless, it's pointing to your innate power. *You can't escape creating reality,* and it's giving you clarity. It's giving you notification, a Facebook notification, a little red flag blip that you can click on and it says, "Hey, this creation is not what you desire." You click on it and it takes you there. You see it and you click "Unfriend" or "Unlike" or "Stop showing up in my newsfeed." That feels good! So you've learned more about who you are and how to master your vibration. Now you go to the Search bar and search for a page that you would really enjoy, that you haven't liked yet—in other words, it's not yet present. So what are your hobbies, or do you have any kind of passion? Don't say "No."

Q: I love to cook.

B: Cook! So you look up this amazing chef on Facebook and you're like, "Wow, this is a really beautiful page; I love this!" and so you Like it and you add it to your newsfeed. If you really love it, you even specify "Every time she posts an update, send me a personal notification." It works that way. Facebook is such a perfect analogy for managing your vibratory state and choosing what you prefer—choosing to see only what you prefer. Do you see that the things that are present in your life are reflections of past vibratory states? And also, to an extent, vibrations that are still lingering or that are still available to you?

Q: I don't know.

B: Or do they seem like random physical events that were out of your control?

Q: Yes.

B: And do you believe that's true? Do you believe that reality consists of an independent physical molecular structure? Or do you believe it's all a dream inside of Consciousness?

Q: I love hearing that it's all dream inside of Consciousness.

B: That's because it's true. You feel good when you hear that, so it must be true. Higher Self agrees with you—that's what good feeling is. Higher Self is always ready to push a button. There's this red button that says "No" and this green button that says "Yes." Whenever you have a thought that is correct, it pushes "Yes!" and you feel good. Whenever you have a thought that feels bad, it's because the thought is untrue, so Higher Self pushes the "No" button and you feel bad. That's how simply the emotional body works; that's all there is to it. No need for psychotherapy! Just recognize that when you feel bad it's because you're thinking something untrue, and when you feel great it is because you're lining up with the true frequency of Existence, the frequency of your true Self. So, if I tell you that everything is a dream inside of Consciousness, does that feel good?

Q: Yes.

B: Nice. You're even smiling—look at you! This smiling is not your delusion, you can't be happy unless your Higher Self agrees with what I'm saying. Do you trust your Higher Self's wisdom? Or do you prefer your own brain-self, linearly-oriented way of seeing the world? You kind of have to make a choice. Do you wish to trust your Higher Self, which means trust what feels good, and say respectfully and appreciatively, "No," to the things that don't feel good. Or, trust what you have grown up with from this very dense physical portion of Creation, taught by your parents, who are nothing but dummies, and then say, "No, I think I am right. Even though my Higher Consciousness sees all infinite parallel realities simultaneously, sees all the parallel lives I'm living right now, what most people call past and future lives, sees all the alternate versions of me that are within my range of possibility and relativity—despite all that, I believe I'm right. So let me feel really bad, because I enjoy that, because I just want to be right."

Q: Your message is very compelling. I do want to trust my Higher Self but I'm not.

B: Compelling. Do you know what compelling is? It's Higher Self pushing the green button! Beep, beep, beep, be-e-e-p, BE-E-E-E-P!!

Q: The wiring needs to be improved.

B: The wiring?

Q: The wiring to the button. The button is being hit but the signal is only slowly getting through.

B: No it's not slow. You feel instantly bad or you feel instantly good. But then you linger. That's up to you. Your free will is honored. You destroy your joy. You hesitate. You base your reality on what you see physically, which is only the representation of your past creations. All these ten principles we've been talking about—you're doing the opposite. Haha! But you're not alone, if that helps.

Q: I know I am not alone.

B: I'm not saying that to encourage you to keep on doing the same thing, but you're not alone. Reacting that way is normal. It's not *natural*, but it's normal. So you have to learn to be *abnormal*. You have to be annoying, you have to be free, you have to wild, rebellious, and adventurous! *You have to be all-in. You have to care about how you feel*, because how you feel is coming from the highest wisdom you have access to as the human brain. The human-based physical mind has *no access* to a consciousness *higher* than, "How do I feel in this moment?" That's as far as our wisdom can reach, in this physical Creation. Through being aware of how you feel, you then become aware of so much more. You become wiser.

This is your guidance mechanism. It should always be honored above any other truth you realize. This is where so many spiritual people go wrong. They take their realizations, and their perspectives on them, above all else. I always say, "You take your personality with you all the way into the realization of the Absolute"—meaning whatever you realize you distort! Whatever you realize, it's still *your point of view* of that realization, which means whatever you realize, it's somewhat distorted.

People idolize their realizations and their inter-
pretations of them. They value them because they
seem so wise and so approved of by gurus with long
beards—gurus who say the same thing and who seem
very authoritative. "Nisargadatta said this, Ramana
Maharshi said this, Buddha said this—so therefore,
I'm right." And they ignore the fact that *it doesn't feel
good! For* example, "Desire should be suppressed; it's
a distraction." Actually, desire is *your only* entrance
point into wisdom, any real type of applicable wisdom. *Don't ever suppress your desires!* Suppress
everything else, but don't suppress your desires, your
integrity, and your respect for other beings' free will.
That and your desire, and you're good to go. Ignore
everything else and you're good to go.

Q: You speak with great certainty.

B: Yes. I don't have a long beard, but I'm just as
authoritative.

Q: I'm not as certain as you are at this moment, but
that doesn't mean I can't be or won't be.

B: Beautiful. Thank you. Doesn't it feel good when
you leave that open?

Q: Yeah, sure.

B: Good, that means it's true.

Q: Yes, I'm trying, I'm looking. And I resonate with your certainty.

B: This is what you're doing right now: imagine a painter's palette with different colors on it. You're exploring the different colors—tasting a little bit here, a little bit there—and you're about to make a choice. You're still exploring your options—which is great, and natural. You're in the process of choosing which color you want to paint your reality with. You have a very explorative energy right now: "What about this? What about that?" That's good! There's an openness there. But just know that you're about to make a choice. Feel free to keep tasting a little bit here and there, but know that nothing is a given—it's up to you.

All of the colors are The One's creation, equally. You can choose blue or red, positive or negative, depression or bliss. The One will only respond, "Oh, thank you! That's another way in which I can express myself." It doesn't experience the depression you experience—it only perceives more of itself. So, it's up to you to choose what feels in alignment with your Higher Self—which, to be clear, is not The One. Higher Self still has preference, it still has a guidance mechanism. It is guiding your theme, it has direct relevance to you, and that should be honored because there's no way to live in the Absolute while you are physical. There's no way to fully become the Absolute One (which you already are on some level) from the physical, because it's not relevant. We're not supposed to. We are physical because we have a purpose, otherwise we would simply not exist in the way that we do.

So, honor your feelings. If something feels good, will you learn to trust that it comes from the highest wisdom you have access to? And if you believe this at some point, ask yourself: "Do I really wish to negotiate with that? Do I really wish to argue with that?" Something feels good, but your belief says, "Well, if I go down this path, my mom or my spouse will no longer love me. So let's not do that.'" But you know that this path feels so good, feels so fulfilling. And you know that it comes from the highest potential wisdom, which has only your best interest in mind. It sees so much more than you do, and it lets you know very clearly through good or bad feelings. Is it really smart to argue with that?

Q: I'm worried that I hesitate, and I still have this tension feeling when I first awake in the morning. It sucks.

B: Then you have let in the first thought without consciously choosing it—one of the ten guidelines I spoke of earlier. But you can still change it; it's still fresh. Choose another thought. What is thought? Thought is simply the means by which you tune into an alternate reality, an alternate state of being. It's not about the thought itself. The thought itself is like the hand that turns the radio dial, tuning into different frequencies. What you want is another frequency— state of being, feeling, conviction, realization. Thought is one means to turn that dial. Use thought and imagination to visualize the things that correspond to your resonance. What would that be for you? What really excites you and puts you on a trajectory of clarity and intention?

Q: Not at this time. I just know I want to feel good.

B: Well, that's specific. You want to feel good. So, how do you do that?

Q: I can manufacture a good feeling. What I've been doing is remembering how great I felt two days ago.

B: Good. You can use your memory, which is a thought, to remember a past state of being and dial back into that vibratory state. Think back to a moment when you felt great. If you do that for a certain period of time, say half a minute, you will start to actually feel that reality once again. Sometimes it may take a little while, depending on how much mess you've generated around that thought, but if the thought becomes very clear, very pure, it can happen instantly, in just a second. This takes a little practice, but for most people 30 seconds will do the trick. You're using thought consciously, right? As a means to tune into a vibratory state that you enjoy? You can always do this. You can always make yourself feel better by thinking things that are in alignment with the way your Higher Self sees reality. The only way to feel good as a human being is to be in alignment with your Higher Self.

Q: By thinking things that are in alignment I am going to feel good?

B: Yes, automatically. Because then your Higher Self is going to press the green button, which is going to send bliss waves your way, endlessly. Higher Self has no limitation; it just depends on how much you're willing to receive? How many exact, precise, abundantly-oriented perspectives do you wish to accumulate in your consciousness? How precisely do you wish to see Existence? How joyful, how blissful, would you like your perspective of this moment to be? It can go as far as you can go—actually, further. You will never run out of bliss, unless you decide that it's enough. Enough is enough!

But that's okay—we get used to it. I say "enough" sometimes. "That was fun, now give me a break. Shit! Okay—a little less bliss, please. Fuck it! No! Aaaaaaaaaahhhh!" You start playing with your frequency, and at some point, you become more and more masterful at it. And then there's no way back. You cannot be fooled; you become your own teacher, your own creator. Does that feel good?

Q: Yes.

B: Are you aligning your thoughts with your Higher Self, right now?

Q: Yes.

B: Good. So, as soon as you feel bad, notice the thought you just had. You were dialing into a reality that is untrue. Wrong thought! Higher Self is kind of like a dictator. It's very precise: "What you're thinking is wrong," It's not a negative thing; that's is just how it works—it's meant to guide you. When you're thinking something wrong, you feel bad. When you are thinking something right, you feel good. How simple do we want it to be?

Question #4

So, what about fear? I have this inspiration to sing, to get up at open mic night and sing. For a minute it feels great, but when the event comes close, I start to feel really scared. So then, I'm like, "Oh, I'm feeling bad, so it must mean I shouldn't do it. I use that as an excuse to not do it. Can you clarify this?

B: Is there anyone else here to which this principle applies right now in your everyday life? Do you have something that you are passionate about, but you're also scared of it, and then you start being confused? Would you mind sharing about it?

Audience member: Well I'm starting to do artwork now and one of the reasons it took me so long to get around to it is that I fear on some level it won't work out, or I won't even enjoy it, or I won't have enough money to get supplies. Often when I desire something, there's fear in there. So I can relate to this question.

B: Yeah, cool. So, for anyone with this experience, can you see it as exciting? Can you see that those thoughts are fun?

At some point, you become so vibrationally oriented that you literally see every physical manifestation as a reflection, as a game. It's an energetic game that you play with yourself. As soon as you see it that way, it becomes much lighter; it becomes a play. So, then you get excited: "Oh, that's a fun thought!" or "Oh, that makes me feel not so good." And then you start navigating. You learn how to ease that vibration into feeling really amazing again, really confident and worthy of whatever it is you desire to do. You open up your flow.

Every time you get excited about a new vision, the Day Two challenge comes up. It can come up in terms of thinking, "I want good art materials, but it costs a lot of money." That's an example of a Day Two challenge, responding to your Day One vision. So, in order to reach the Day Three confirmation, transformation, celebration, you need to approach Day Two with the playfulness of Day One energy. For example, "I really want to do my art, no matter what. I know that somehow it's possible, but now this thought has come up, which makes me feel it's not. It makes me feel negative and heavy." If you approach this with excitement like, "Oh, fun! I'm feeling not-so-good. What is it? What's the belief? Oh, there it is! If I buy this set of paints, I'll have to cut back on my food expenses. I also need new canvases and other stuff. At some point, I might run out of money. I need to figure something out with my rent or maybe get a job of some kind."

In other words, the mind goes off into its rationality, based on being physically focused. Physicality will always show you limitation, because it is only one snapshot of infinite possibilities. One snapshot never contains any other reality. In other words, this room does not contain China; this room only contains this room. If you go to China, you'll experience China. If you base your reality on what's here in this room, you'll never believe China is possible. But if you simply *think* of China, then suddenly you'll see an advertisement—because Amazon is so smart it can read your vibration. Amazon will place a sidebar ad says, "Want to go to China?" And you're like, "Fuck! I better watch what I'm thinking! But yes, thank you Amazon." And you hit the button and book your flight to China—all because you were in an upward spiraling energy of "anything is possible"—not based on just what you see in this room.

If I base everything on just this room, then I'll never get out of this room, right? So, if we state definitions to ourselves, like "I can't do this, I'm not worthy of it, it's not going to happen, I don't have the means," they're all based on the physical focus. In the non-physical focus, which to us is imagination, there are infinite means.

Imagine infinite means, infinite money. What does that look like? What does it feel like? Imagination allows for infinite means; it has nothing to do with your current "reality," with the structure of this room. So your definitions change from fearful to *exciting*: "What I enjoy is the *imagining* of infinite money, or infinite trips to China, or infinite pencils to draw with and infinite artwork to sell and enjoy and to share with people. I enjoy my own inspired process, of being in that channeling-intuitive state while doing my art work. I'm really looking forward to that! That's all that matters to me. So, I'm going to ease myself back into that vibratory state of conviction, every single time a limiting thought is pushed to the surface. The limiting thought *wants* to be seen and transformed—that's why it comes up! It doesn't come up because it's a real concern; it comes up because it is an *unreal* concern."

Concerns come up when you increase your frequency *precisely because* they are unreal concerns. They need to be seen because you're still believing in unreal things. If you're holding on to unreal beliefs, you can't increase your frequency past a certain point. So when you move past that threshold, everything that doesn't fit that new reality will disappear. But if it's something that you're holding onto subconsciously, then it needs to show up. If you didn't hold onto any negative belief past a certain threshold of vibration, then you would simply go up to that vibration. There would be no challenge—no Day Two doubts would arise.

It's exciting! It is a vibrational game. Get excited about it, and *be all-in!* You want this more than anything, so you *want* these doubts to come up. What you're most interested in is not painting or being worthy of showing your artwork, or performing music. What you're interested in is the way you live life, the way you feel right now. That's why it's exciting when doubts come up; that's why it's exciting when things aren't happening the way you want. *It's exciting because it's an opportunity to master your state of being even more.*

So, you say, "Thank you. I know I'm infinitely worthy; I know I'm infinitely abundant. Eventually, I'll get what I want anyway, so there's no rush, no time pressure. I already have what I desire— otherwise it wouldn't pop up in my frequency. Now there's this little hiatus, this little gap, this little doubt that comes up. I want to see this doubt! I'm really excited to see it because I'm a vibrational being, and I wish to clear up my vibration so I can enjoy even greater degrees of wisdom, bliss, joy, love, service, and connection to The One in my everyday life. So, thank you for showing me I have limiting ideas. I so appreciate it, I so want this! I'm not afraid of temporarily seeing and feeling the negative energy of this doubt. I know it's only temporary, and the more I look at it and appreciate it, the quicker it will dissolve. I will ease it back into the vibrational conviction that I am infinitely worthy, infinitely capable, infinitely abundant, and inseparable from All That Is."

Question #5

Q: Last week I sat up here and I was a little worried about the nuclear situation. For some reason, I've appointed myself to be in charge of—at least light-heartedly—getting rid of all the nuclear weapons on planet Earth. It is fun for me to imagine that I might actually have some influence in that. So, we had this little talk last week, and you know, Putin kind of calmed down a bit and things are a little more peaceful there...

B: Good to know!

Q: I think you helped, I think everybody here helped. So I want to keep going with it. Personally, I want to experience Heaven on Earth. **My question is what should I think about before I go to sleep tonight? I think I already know, but please tell me.**

B: Well what would you say?

Q: I'd say I should pre-program the kind of dream I want to have.

B: Well, that's lovely. You can also do it in your waking life. What should you think about? The answer is always *whatever feels best*. If you think something completely unrelated to the issue you think you're working on, but it gives you a great amount of joy and expansion, that's going to help you manifest your project—assuming it is actually what's relevant for you, assuming it is actually desired. It might just be a substitute desire, but if it's a relevant, true desire, it will come about by thinking of something completely unrelated that brings you a great sense of joy and empowerment.

On the other hand, if you think about the thing you wish to create, even visualizing the positive outcome of it for many people, it may still generate some straining, because there's such a charge and attachment to that particular outcome. "Yeah, it's going to look great.... maybe it's not going to look great...no, it's going to look great and it feels good..." You're thinking positively, but you also think that maybe it won't happen because there are so many things involved. So you're sending out a semi-negative vibration, even though you are positively thinking about the very thing you think you want to establish. This is actually *less* effective than feeling great joy in thinking about a frog hopping around.

Somehow it will all figure itself out. Don't worry about the how's and the when's of manifestation. Trust in your Higher Self's ability to create. You're not creating with your physical molecules, you're generating from your Higher Consciousness' ability to manifest this dream into physicality. You have to give up trying to change physical reality and take on your right to be a vibrational co-creator. Give up believing that you're physically making things happen. You make things happen through thoughts, through connecting vibrationally to parallel realities using imagination. So, think of something that brings you the greatest amount of joy, and Putin will put down his arms. Do you believe this is how this system works, and are you willing to ease out of your strong intention a little bit to get this thing done?

Q: Yeah, because it's really a pain in the butt.

B: Yes, I imagine to single-handedly remove all nuclear weapons from planet Earth would be a pain in the butt. You can actually do it, but not by being overly focused on it. That's the irony. You need to manage your vibration. If you manage your vibratory state—in other words, if you always feel good and confident—you will shift into the parallel reality where there are no nuclear weapons. You are already in a reality where no nuclear war can ever happen again, just so you know. But, if you still want to clean it up, you can do so. There's no actual reason to clean it up, no physical reason, unless it is your joy to do so, unless it resonates to do so. If that's the case, then please keep doing it. But the way for you to actually manifest this is to ease yourself into the state that feels the truest and most passionate to you.

I totally admire your vision, and I think you should go for it. Make sure you feel good while you're doing it. If thinking about it makes you really, really, ecstatic, if it's charge-free when you think of all the nuclear weapons having been disposed of, then great. On the other hand, if it feels good, but what comes up is, "Oh yeah... but it's never going to happen because of this or that..." then clean that up. And also, see what negative belief is underneath it, some negative belief that does not believe in the outcome. Or think of something completely different that brings you 100% holistic, blissful connection to your True Self. That will be even *more* efficient. The next day you will wake up and read in the newspaper that something was put in motion that removed some country's nuclear weapons. So, you're not creating physically, you're generating through consciousness, through vibration.

Question #6

Q: I'm glad you showed up from wherever you came from, because I want to do this kind of thing with music and take people into really high states of emotion. **I want help with getting the money to do it. I'm still struggling with money.** If we had Warren Buffet sitting here with us, we would be getting a lot more attention. How do we do that?

B: Well, success creates more success. Justin Bieber is the perfect example. He is only successful because he was successful. It's like he is successful, and therefore, he becomes more successful. Anything you have that you're pouring yourself into generates more and more, and it amplifies. So yes, confidence will always be king. Confidence in whatever is relevant for you. If that is to generate music that uplifts people— whatever it is, do it as confidently as you can. The confidence and the purity of that moment will generate more and more and more of it.

This is also how the universe works. It doubles and triples and quadruples the effects every single time you add to that idea, to that excitement—as long as it still has a vibrational relevance for you, and you feel the emotional state or the state-of-being nature of the thought you are having. The first time you have a new idea you may just think the thought casually,

"Oh, there's another option I could take..." You consider it as part of what could be possible for you and you feel out whether you like the idea or not. The second time you think that thought, it is made specific and it is made yours; it starts to become intentional and the thought gathers strength and momentum. The third time you think that thought, it doubles the power-effect of the second time. The fourth time, it doubles the power-effect of the third time, and so on. That's why repetition of the most important realizations and ideas and feelings is so powerful. Focus on what you desire repeatedly in your everyday life.

So, initially you're just throwing it out there. It's a random thought and doesn't really do anything other than expand your mind to a new possibility. The second time you think it—boom! It starts to become specific, it starts to create a Law of Attraction effect towards you. The third time it doubles the effects, and so on. But this should not become, "Let me think it, think it, and think it!" Because again, what's most important is that you feel good, right? So at some point, if it feels stale, think something else. Always plant new seeds. At some point a particular seed, a particular imagination, is finished. It feels like, "Oh okay, now it's up to Higher Self, so at some point it will become physical. I'm not going to sit here in a waiting vibration, which feels really bad, actually. No.

What's the next most exciting thing I can imagine, focus on and/or take action on?"

The next most exciting thing can be completely unrelated—don't limit yourself to one passion or to the idea of a linear process of progression. Go explore, go expand yourself! You will have no idea who you are until you start really tapping into your imagination. Then, before you know it, you're interested in all kinds of things, both physical and nonphysical. It's lovely to be interested in physical things again, and also in non-physical things. It is lovely to be excited. Because you know it's all a game. because you know Consciousness can't die, because you know it doesn't matter—so why not play in accordance with your alignment? Why not generate visions that bring you so much bliss, so much joy, and be a powerful example for other people to match that vibration in themselves. Then we will actually end up living like Heaven on Earth. Why not? It's fun.

*   *   *   *   *

Goodnight everyone. Sweet dreams and sweet waking dreams. Generate, be conscious, be aware of your vibration and choose yours. I love you

A Note from the Team

To help us achieve our mission of an Enlightened Civilization for All by 2035, please consider leaving a positive review of this book on its Amazon page and recommend it to your circles.

Afterword

By Bentinho Massaro

Inundate yourself...

I often recommend ways to make the journey to enlightenment and empowerment easier for people. One of the fastest methods is to inundate and surround yourself with quality reminders, pointers, and instructional materials. On a daily basis we are dealing with huge amounts of unconsciousness within us and around us, so it's crucial that we remind ourselves and prioritize our alignment and awareness.

In short: It's easy to forget who we truly are, so let's put some tools in place to help us remember.

In this age of the internet and of technology in general, it has become easier than ever before to achieve something as previously obscure as Buddhahood/enlightenment—and in addition to that, an empowered (super) human life. Through our own dedication and focus—with a little help from the reminders that we can put in our environment—we can all realize the eternal bliss that is our nature, and learn to effectively utilize the power of our free will.

This is the simple advice I frequently give: whenever you're not feeling particularly aligned or powerful, there's actually no easier way to raise your vibration than to just make yourself watch a bunch of my videos or read a few pages of my work (or a similarly empowering work you resonate with), and do it right in that moment.

The focus of my teachings has always been to synthesize complex spiritual truths and present them in simple, practical, and uplifting terms—to speed up your journey. So to make your own path easier, please give yourself the gift of exploring the links provided below.

With love,
Bentinho

Additional Resources

Stay Connected

BentinhoMassaro.com —
Bentinho Massaro's general website offers a good introduction to him and his work. Read some of the blog articles, **sign up for his newsletter**, and check out his upcoming events.

TrinfinityAcademy.com —
This is Bentinho's definitive work—and a world's first. Trinfinity Academy is a (now free) online course for enlightenment and empowerment. It is a truly comprehensive, yet accessible, resource and home for the sincere spiritual seeker who wants to go in-depth with the most profound spiritual and empowering realizations available to humanity today. The Academy guides the seeker step-by-step, making the impossible seem easy to achieve, regardless of where one is in the spiritual journey. It will save you decades of otherwise confused and convoluted seeking. Please, take this unique opportunity and explore Trinfinity Academy.

Trinfinity Academy's courses were gifted to the world for free as of September 30, 2016, as an additional incentive from Bentinho to make this platform a worldwide phenomenon that can serve millions, instead of thousands.

Dive in, expand, ascend, enjoy, fall in love with your existence and share your favorite lessons and courses with your circle of friends. Pass it forward: recommend Trinfinity Academy frequently, blog about it, share it on social media platforms—and thus help us achieve an Enlightened Civilization by 2035.

Facebook.com/BentinhoMassaro —

At the time of this writing, Bentinho continues to personally create and post the vast majority of his Facebook updates. He currently uses Facebook as his main platform from which to reach the largest number of people. So, make sure you "like" and follow his page for daily updates, quotes, spontaneous and personal live stream moments, and additional resources.

Bentinho Massaro's Teaching and Community —
Facebook.com/groups/336863633071053
If you're not yet a member of this community, type the above name in the Facebook search bar and request to join this group. This is a community of 15,000 dedicated people who love to explore and embody Bentinho's work. Join us, create with us, question with us, explore with us, and occasionally

get your questions answered directly by Bentinho. This group is also sometimes the first place (or the only place) where certain news is shared.

Youtube.com/BentinhoMassaro —

Browse and subscribe to Bentinho Massaro's official YouTube channel. Watch and enjoy hundreds of hours of valuable material, and consider frequently sharing links to videos with your circle of friends.

Trinfinity Corp. —

Trinfinity.us

Learn more about the corporation founded by Bentinho with the mission of co-creating an Enlightened Civilization by the year 2035 ready for interstellar citizenship. At the time of this writing, the primary purpose of this website is to generate funding for our various projects and plans by which Trinfinity aims to achieve this ambitious—but totally achievable—goal.

Email —

contact@bentinhomassaro.com
BentinhoMassaro.com/contact

Bentinho Massaro

By Janet Marchant

Bentinho Massaro is an unusual being. You could say he is extra-ordinary, having integrated the "extra"—or non-physical—levels of his consciousness into his human experience. He calls this True Simultaneity, and he claims we can all learn to expand and live in this way.

Since his first enlightenment experiences as a teenager, Bentinho has been riding the waves of an intensely awakened life. He started teaching at age 18 and today he is an internationally recognized spiritual teacher and empowerment speaker who holds retreats in major US and European cities.

Even as a child, growing up in Holland, Bentinho had a sense of the unlimited possibilities within human consciousness. At age 14, he had the clear realization that the veil of being a "person" had fallen over him, creating a sense of separation from Life. He resolved to go beyond the veil to find the Truth of his own being and to discover the actual workings of life that would liberate humanity from conflict and suffering.

He began a relentless quest, exploring all kinds of teachers, philosophies, and methods—staying with each practice only long enough to digest what was useful to his goal. Eventually exhausted, he realized that all the spiritual "authorities" were no more enlightened than himself, and he made a radical decision: to follow only his own resonance and trust his intuition without hesitation. It was in India, at age 18, that he realized full enlightenment: the always, already here God-Presence/Pure Awareness.

"I sank into indescribable freedom that knows no boundary," he says. "This enlightenment was the end of an unpleasant dream of separation, and the beginning of my true life as an awakened consciousness."

This background of focused seeking helps explain an extraordinary creation that Bentinho launched in late 2014—an online university for enlightenment that many (former) seekers claim is the quickest available way to achieve actual, *experiential* Self-Realization. He named it Trinfinity Academy to indicate the three categories of his teachings: Enlightenment, Empowerment, and Infinity. Because it offers and *can deliver to anyone who wants it* a fully enlightened life, I view the Academy as a historical first—that will play a role in the transition of humanity to a more enlightened era.

Yet Bentinho says he is just getting started, even though creating the Academy was, at one point, the goal of his life. A new and ambitious vision for planet Earth and human civilization has opened up to him. His overarching mission, in his own words, is *"to establish a 100% enlightened civilization—that is then also ready for interstellar absorption—by the year 2035."*

Bentinho continues to refine and simplify his teachings with a goal to reach people from every walk of life, building a bridge to enlightenment and self-empowerment for the "average Joe," not just for those already in the spiritual community. "It's what I came here for," he says.

On a personal level, Bentinho embodies the fully passionate lifestyle that he teaches—including "free-solo" rock-climbing (no ropes) and free-diving to depths over 130 feet on a single breath. Currently he is exploring new roles as entrepreneur, CEO, inventor, and investor, adding to previous skills as Reiki master, yogi, telekinetic, and polyphasic sleeper. He also occasionally enjoys a fine whiskey with a cigar.

CPSIA information can be obtained
at www.ICGtesting.com
Printed in the USA
LVOW12s1009201216
518081LV00003B/191/P